PEGASUS BRIDGE

Bénouville D-Day 1944

WILL FOWLER

First published in Great Britain in 2010 by Osprey Publishing,
Midland House, West Way, Botley, Oxford, OX2 0PH, UK
44–02 23rd St, Suite 219, Long Island City, NY 11101, USA
E-mail: info@ospreypublishing.com

Print ISBN: 978 1 84603 848 8
PDF e-book ISBN: 978 1 84908 287 7

Page layout by: Bounford.com, Cambridge, UK
Index by Alan Thatcher
Typeset in Sabon
Maps by Bounford.com, Cambridge, UK
BEVs by Alan Gilliland
Originated by PPS Grasmere Ltd, Leeds, UK
Printed in China through Worldprint

10 11 12 13 14   10 9 8 7 6 5 4 3 2 1

A CIP catalogue record for this book is available from the British Library

THE WOODLAND TRUST

Osprey Publishing are supporting the Woodland Trust, the UK's leading
woodland conservation charity, by funding the dedication of trees.

IMPERIAL WAR MUSEUM COLLECTIONS

Many of the photos in this book come from the Imperial War Museum's
huge collections which cover all aspects of conflict involving Britain and
the Commonwealth since the start of the twentieth century. These rich
resources are available online to search, browse and buy at
www.iwmcollections.org.uk. In addition to Collections Online, you can
visit the Visitor Rooms where you can explore over 8 million photographs,
thousands of hours of moving images, the largest sound archive of its
kind in the world, thousands of diaries and letters written by people in
wartime, and a huge reference library. To make an appointment, call (020)
7416 5320, or e-mail mail@iwm.org.uk.

Imperial War Museum www.iwm.org.uk

DEDICATION

To the soldiers of The Rifles killed on operations in Iraq and Afghanistan –
Swift and Bold.

FOR A CATALOGUE OF ALL BOOKS PUBLISHED BY OSPREY MILITARY
AND AVIATION PLEASE CONTACT:

Osprey Direct, c/o Random House Distribution Center,
400 Hahn Road, Westminster, MD 21157
Email: uscustomerservice@ospreypublishing.com

Osprey Direct, The Book Service Ltd, Distribution Centre,
Colchester Road, Frating Green, Colchester, Essex, CO7 7DW
E-mail: customerservice@ospreypublishing.com

www.ospreypublishing.com

CONTENTS

INTRODUCTION

To the young German soldier and his comrade, standing guard on the bridge across the shipping canal at Bénouville in Normandy early on the morning of 6 June 1944, it seemed as if a flak-damaged Allied bomber had crashed on the far bank. An aircraft of some type had certainly come hurtling down from the cloudy night sky and ploughed across the ground towards the eastern end of the bridge.

What 18-year-old Pte Helmut Romer, an easy-going big city boy from Berlin, did not realize was that he had become the first German soldier to witness D-Day, the Allied invasion of Normandy. The crashing aircraft was in fact the first of three troop-carrying gliders, and the bridge he was guarding was the objective of a company of highly trained and superbly led British soldiers of the Oxfordshire and Buckinghamshire Light Infantry. Moments after the landing, these soldiers had charged out of the gliders, stormed across the bridge, suppressed the defences and captured this key D-Day objective, all in about ten minutes.

In the 21st century, the 'Realities of War' training programme, devised for junior soldiers at the British Army Foundation College (AFC) at Harrogate, takes young men and women to the battlefields of Normandy. It is an opportunity for these 16- and 17-year-olds to see the places where in the summer of 1944, men, some only a little older than themselves, fought against a tough, well-equipped and battle-hardened enemy. Among the sites they visit are this bridge at Bénouville and another bridge about half a mile away across the River Orne. Today these are known respectively as Pegasus Bridge and Horsa Bridge, and the author is one of several Royal British Legion guides who have had the privilege of taking the young soldiers from AFC Harrogate to this unique battleground.

The soldiers who assaulted and captured the bridges in the early hours of the morning of D-Day, the Allied landings in Normandy on 6 June 1944, had been delivered to their objective by Horsa gliders. Today the officers and NCO staff from Harrogate, many of them veterans of operational tours in Iraq and Afghanistan, compare the Horsa gliders to the Chinook helicopter, the workhorse troop transport in these theatres. What distinguishes yesterday's Horsas from today's Chinooks is that once the glider pilots had started the descent flight to the landing zone (LZ) in 1944, there was no going back: pilots, glider and troops on board were committed to action – it was a one-way ride to death or glory. They were also making this hazardous landing without any of the sophisticated night vision aids available to pilots today – to land a Horsa at night, the pilots had only the 'Mark 1 Eyeball'.

The Café Gondrée, the first house to be liberated on D-Day and the Company Clearing Station in the fighting that followed, and now run by Arlette Gondrée, the daughter of the original owners. She continues a tradition of hospitality for British soldiers, both serving and veterans, that was begun at dawn on 6 June 1944. (WF)

To be exact, the glider-borne assault and capture of the two bridges was not a raid but a *coup de main*, a surprise attack launched to capture and hold a single key target. A raid would, for example, have seen troops capture and demolish the bridges and then withdraw. Here the tiny force captured and held the bridges until they were relieved by paratroops.

Soon after the capture of the bridges, ACM Sir Trafford Leigh-Mallory said of the incredibly accurate landing by the glider pilots that it was probably the finest feat of flying in World War II – a true compliment, coming from a very senior and often very critical RAF officer to young NCO glider pilots, all of whom were soldiers.

ORIGINS

The landings at Pegasus Bridge grew out of the wider planning for D-Day – a process that had begun almost as soon as the British Expeditionary Force (BEF) had been forced out of France in 1940 and evacuated from the beaches of Dunkirk.

The Normandy beaches to the west of the River Orne had been identified as a possible area for a landing. Most of them were areas of flat, open sand on which landing craft could beach safely, and tanks, guns and vehicles could land. The south coast of England had several large ports that would accommodate troops and shipping before the invasion. Finally, the beaches were within range of single-engined fighters operating from airfields on the British mainland.

Aware that the French coast facing England was the most likely site for an invasion, the Germans had begun building coastal defences as far back as 1942. The main weight of defences lay around the ports and along the coast opposite Dover – the shortest route across the English Channel, and consequently the most logical area for an invasion force to land.

Both the British and the Americans had seen the success of German airborne forces in the opening years of World War II and were quick to see their potential. Intense selection and training programmes were instituted, and soon both nations had formidable airborne forces. Men could be delivered to battle by parachute (paratroops) or by glider (airborne).

The British adopted the distinctive maroon beret for airborne forces; at one stage the newly formed Special Air Service (SAS) was required to swap its distinctive sand-coloured berets for maroon. While the Parachute Regiment had its own distinctive cap badge of a winged parachute surmounted by a crown, older air-landing formations retained their regimental cap badges, and the Oxfordshire and Buckinghamshire Light Infantry's silver bugle horn badge was backed with a rifle-green patch. On their battledress tunics the men sported the striking Pegasus insignia.

In the summer of 1942 LtGen 'Boy' Browning, appointed as Commander of the 1st Airborne Division, asked the distinguished artist Edward (later Major) Seago to design an emblem for the airborne forces. In October that year Seago produced a classic design, a maroon square upon which was the outline in pale blue of the mythical Greek warrior Bellerophon riding the winged horse Pegasus.

Normally, both parachutes and gliders were used in major operations since gliders could carry heavy weapons and vehicles such as jeeps, anti-tank guns and even the Tetrarch light tank. The attraction of the glider, which the Luftwaffe had demonstrated at the modern Belgian fort of Eben Emael in 1940, was that like today's troop-lift helicopter, it could put down a formed group – normally of platoon strength – on a compact landing zone. The British required their glider pilots not only to deliver men and equipment safely into battle, but also to join them on the ground to fight as infantry following the landing. Paratroops were less vulnerable but could be scattered by the wind or the speed at which they exited from the aircraft, or both. It could take time for a group of paratroops to form up and become an effective fighting force.

The drawback of gliders was that they were very vulnerable, being made from light materials such as fabric and wood. While some might crash, killing and wounding the occupants, others could be raked with small-arms fire as they approached the landing zone.

Despite this drawback, from as early as 1940 the British had begun development of the Horsa troop- and cargo-carrying glider, to meet War Department specification

X.26/40. The first Airspeed Horsa made its maiden flight on 12 September 1941. The specification stated that the gliders were to be built in a number of sections, using facilities not needed for more urgent aircraft production, and as a result manufacture was spread across separate factories, which limited the likely loss from air raids.

The glider was a high-wing cantilever monoplane with wooden wings and a wooden semi-monocoque fuselage. The fuselage was built in three sections bolted together: the front was the pilot's compartment and main freight-loading door; the centre section was accommodation for troops or freight; the rear supported the tail unit. Airspeed subcontracted construction to Austin Motors and, since much of the airframe was made of wood, work also went to furniture manufacturers such as Harris Lebus.

The Horsa glider was one of the first to have a tricycle undercarriage. On operational flights this could be jettisoned after take-off and the landing made on a sprung skid under the fuselage. The wings had large 'barn door' flaps that allowed the pilot to make a steep, high rate of descent landing and consequently put the glider down in a very confined landing zone. There were two pilots, who sat in side-by-side seats with dual controls. Aft of the pilot's compartment on the port side was the hinged cargo-loading door, which doubled as a loading ramp. The main compartment could accommodate 15 soldiers and their equipment on bench seats along the sides. Besides the cargo door, they could enter and exit from a smaller door on the starboard side. On landing, the fuselage joint at the rear end of the main section could be broken to assist in rapid unloading. There were stories of soldiers so eager to exit the glider and unload the stores that they were already starting to unbolt this section as the glider started its final descent.

A Horsa could also carry six Central Landing Establishment (CLE) equipment containers fitted under the wings. The later AS.58 Horsa II had a hinged nose section, reinforced floor and double nose wheels to support the extra weight of vehicles. The tow was attached to the nose-wheel strut, rather than the dual wing points as in the Horsa I. By the end of World War II a total of 3,655 Horsas had been built and at D-Day there were about 1,000 available for operations.

The operational debut of the Horsa was during the landings on Sicily in Operation *Husky* in July 1943. So that the gliders could be available at airfields in North Africa, the pilots had to make a long and incredibly hazardous journey under tow from their bases in southern England. A number of factors contributed to the airborne operation suffering high casualties, with some gliders being cast off by their tug aircraft too far from the coast and ditching in the rough sea at night. Other aircraft had been fired on by Allied anti-aircraft gunners, who had mistakenly assumed they were under a low-level Luftwaffe attack.

Many lessons were learned from *Husky* and by D-Day new drills were in place to ensure that as far as possible there was no repetition of those tragic mistakes. One of these would be implemented dramatically on all Allied aircraft operating over Normandy – including the gliders. Wings and fuselages were painted in bold black and white stripes – D-Day stripes. Allied anti-aircraft gunners were instructed that no aircraft with these markings were to be engaged.

On D-Day, British, Canadian and American paratroops and airborne forces would secure the flanks of the amphibious landings, capturing and holding key ground and access routes near the beaches. To the west, men of the 101st and 82nd Airborne Divisions would ensure that soldiers of the 4th Division of the US VIII Corps were able to push inland from Utah Beach along the causeways across the flooded fields that blocked the exits off the beach. To the east, the British 6th Airborne

HORSA GLIDER

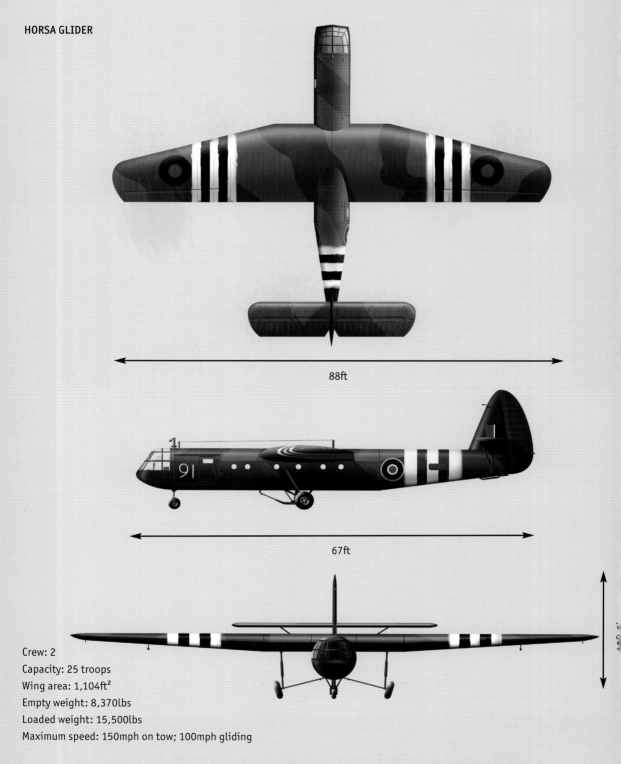

88ft

67ft

Crew: 2
Capacity: 25 troops
Wing area: 1,104ft²
Empty weight: 8,370lbs
Loaded weight: 15,500lbs
Maximum speed: 150mph on tow; 100mph gliding

The Airspeed Horsa I glider had a maximum take-off weight of 15,500lbs. With the Horsa II this rose to 15,750lbs. However, in all operations with the prospect of no immediate resupply, the troops would attempt to carry as much ammunition as possible. The Horsa I was 67ft long and the II 11in longer. The Horsa II had a hinged nose for direct loading of vehicles and guns.

Division would capture the high ground to the east of Sword Beach, where the 3rd Division of the British 1st Corps would be landing. FM Bernard Montgomery, who had been appointed to command the 21st Army Group of the Anglo-American forces who would land on D-Day, had insisted that the invasion force should be increased and that Sword was vital if the German 15th Army was not to contain the beachhead and prevent a break-out.

One factor that could allow the German 711th Division and 21st Panzer Division to contain the British beachhead was the Canal de Caen à la Mer ('Canal from Caen to the Sea'), more commonly known simply as the Caen Canal. This ship canal with locks connected the inland city of Caen and its docks with the town of Ouistreham on the Channel coast. If defended, it would be a formidable obstacle, being 9 miles long and in places 33ft deep. Work on its construction had begun in 1837 and the canal was opened in August that year and deepened in 1920. The canal was an obstacle – but there was worse. To the east was the tidal River Orne; at low tide shelving banks of deep mud were exposed. Like the Caen Canal, if the river was defended it would be difficult to cross without suffering heavy casualties.

The lowest bridging point across the river and canal was at the small hamlet of Bénouville. At the canal there was a *bascule* or swing bridge, built in 1934, which had a heavy counterweight that allowed it to be quickly raised so that shipping could pass along the canal. The River Orne was spanned by a *pont tournant*, a narrow single-lane bridge that pivoted on a central stone pier, which had been designed by the famous French engineer Gustave Eiffel.

On the left bank of the canal an enterprising Frenchman had built a café, the Buvette du Tramway – an ideal spot to serve travellers waiting for ships to negotiate that stretch of the canal when the bridge was raised, and originally a stop on a tramway that linked Caen to the coast. In 1934 it was bought by Georges and Thérèse Gondrée and renamed 'Café Gondrée'. The café had a large garden where they were able to grow fruit and vegetables. By 1944, they and their two daughters, Georgette and Arlette, had endured 1,450 days of occupation and the unwelcome company of a German garrison and defences around the bridge. To the garrison, the Gondrées seemed to be a simple family business that sold drinks and snacks. For the Germans, one of the best features of the café was that the guard commander could keep watch on the bridge from the comfort of an indoor table.

However, far from being unsophisticated rural folk, the Gondrées were quiet members of the Resistance and would prove to be a valuable source of intelligence for the Allies. Thérèse Gondrée came from Alsace and consequently understood German, while Georges had worked for 12 years as a clerk in Lloyds Bank in Paris and understood English. Thérèse listened to the NCOs chatting in the café and reported anything of value to Georges, who passed it on to Mme Vion, the director of the Château de Bénouville, a big maternity hospital to the south of Bénouville. The director in turn told it to Resistance contacts in Caen on her trips to the city for medical supplies. From Caen the information was transmitted by clandestine radio or carried in RAF Lysander liaison aircraft, which made hazardous night flights to improvised airstrips in France. The maternity hospital was also used by Mme Vion to hide downed Allied aircrew who had evaded capture and were on the run. Mme Vion used the hospital's ambulances to move them on to other safe houses.

On 2 June, Georges had passed on a vital piece of intelligence that Thérèse had overheard: the firing point for the demolition charges on the bridge was located in the machine-gun bunker on the left bank of the canal. Allied planners knew that if these bridges were captured it would deny the German forces swift access to the left flank of the Allied invasion and would, moreover, allow the men landing at Sword

JULY 1943

Operational debut of Horsa glider during Operation *Husky* in Sicily.

9

The elegant *pont tournant* across the River Orne designed by the famous French engineer Gustave Eiffel. The German traffic sign on the left, erected in February 1941, bans civilian vehicles except bicycles. (IWM B5230)

Beach to break out to the south and east to link up with the airborne forces landing on drop zones across the river.

Air photo-reconnaissance, as well as information from the Resistance, was collated at the 6th Airborne Division Headquarters at Brigmerston House on Salisbury Plain in Wiltshire, codenamed 'Broadmoor' and better known to the soldiers simply as 'the Mad House' – after the Broadmoor psychiatric hospital. The Allied planners had a wealth of detail, and the map of the area, which, like all D-Day documents, was given a new super-secret classification, 'Bigot', showed the bridge and its defences and those of other enemy positions in the vicinity. Those officers who were cleared to study this material were designated as 'Bigoted'.

Intelligence had established that the bridges were defended by a 50-strong garrison of the 736th Grenadier Regiment 716th Infantry Division, who were believed to be conscripts from occupied countries but with a stiffening of German NCOs and officers. They were commanded by Maj Hans Schmidt. The main defences for the canal bridge were on the east bank and included a static anti-tank gun in a concrete weapons pit or Tobruk stand. Trenches radiated from this position, as they did from the bunker across the road. A simple movable barbed wire barrier was sited on the west bank with a machine gun in a sandbagged position. The river bridge was less heavily guarded but had a bunker and a machine gun in a weapons pit on the east bank. It appeared that the German garrison anticipated that an attack would come from the east and had taken precautions against this.

Although it was becoming increasingly obvious to the German high command in western Europe that an invasion was imminent, and Schmidt had been told that the two bridges were one of the most critical points in Normandy, his men were not 'stood to' on full alert on 6 June and, moreover, nor was he. He was up the road in Ranville, where he may have settled down for the night in his accommodation, a requisitioned house, though one version of events has him enjoying an evening with his French girlfriend. Except for the two sentries on each bridge, his troops were either asleep in their bunkers, or dozing in their slit trenches or in the machine-gun bunker, or enjoying late night hospitality in Bénouville.

Until not long before, the Germans had believed that the major threat to the bridges was the French Resistance, who had targeted road and rail links to sabotage German operations in France. Maj Schmidt had orders to blow the bridges if capture seemed imminent. However, he felt that if the charges were in place they might either be detonated by the Resistance or simply neutralized. It seemed prudent, therefore, to store the charges in a bunker, and, since his bridges were almost 5 miles from the coast, he reasoned that in the event of an amphibious landing, he would have plenty of warning before any Allied ground forces reached them. He would have time to prepare the bridges, blow them up and then hold the area. Schmidt saw himself as a loyal German but like many men – non-political Germans and dedicated Nazis alike – he had grown soft in France.

On the night of 5/6 June at Vimont, east of Caen, a German colonel was in his headquarters working on personnel reports. Oberst Hans von Luck, commanding the 125th Panzer Grenadier Regiment of the 21st Panzer Division, would potentially pose the greatest threat to the British attack on the bridges. Von Luck was a veteran of the campaigns in Poland, France and the Eastern Front, where in the bitter winter of 1941 he and his troops had reached the outer suburbs of Moscow. His experience of the war in North Africa had left him with a respect for the British that bordered on affection: in the years after 1945 this would grow and a strong bond would be formed with John Howard and the men of the Oxfordshire and Buckinghamshire Light Infantry.

The 21st Panzer Division was Rommel's favourite division and within it Von Luck's regiment, the 125th, was one of the best equipped. The original division had fought in North Africa, suffered heavy losses at El Alamein and during the fighting withdrawal to Tunisia, and was virtually destroyed in May 1943 at the end of the campaign in Africa. As with the units lost at Stalingrad, Hitler hated the idea that they no longer existed and had been removed from the order of battle, and so 21st Panzer Division was re-formed in Normandy in July 1943 with about 2,000 survivors of the original division. They were initially equipped with modified French Hotchkiss and Somua tanks that had been captured in 1940. A year later they had received their first PzKpfw IV tanks. In 1944, the division would suffer heavy losses in the defence of Caen and the fighting in the Falaise Pocket. On D-Day, however, it would be the only formation to launch a serious counterattack against the Allies and, in so doing, get close to splitting Juno and Sword beaches and reaching the sea.

An oblique aerial reconnaissance photograph taken on 24 March 1944. To the left is the Caen Canal and on the right are the paler waters of the River Orne. The road between the two bridges would offer the paratroops and glider-borne soldiers some degree of security after the bridges had been secured. Howard's plan ensured that his forces were concentrated on the 'island' formed by the canal and river. (Museum of Army Flying)

INITIAL STRATEGY

The operation to capture the two bridges across the Caen Canal and the Orne, codenamed Operation *Deadstick*, would demonstrate that ordinary men can be capable of extraordinary courage and exemplary leadership. The force was made up of a reinforced company of the Oxfordshire and Buckinghamshire Light Infantry (widely known as the Ox and Bucks), and its leader was Maj John Howard.

John Howard had joined the King's Shropshire Light Infantry (KSLI) in 1932. He remembered his early days in recruit training as an unhappy period of homesickness but he soldiered on and served for six years. He applied for a commission but, though he had the right educational qualifications, as a private soldier in the inter-war army, he was rejected; he was, however, made up to Corporal. It may be that this initial rejection was a spur to his ambition to prove himself not only as a soldier but as a commanding officer. He left the army and became a constable in the Oxford City Police. At the outbreak of the war he was recalled to the KSLI with his rank of Corporal; however, with his pre-war experience and maturity, he saw rapid promotion, rising to Company Sergeant Major (CSM). Within five months of rejoining the colours he had reached the pinnacle of non-commissioned ranks – WO1, Regimental Sergeant Major (RSM). He was offered a commission and went to an Officer Cadet Training Unit (OCTU) in mid-1940. On being commissioned, he joined the Ox and Bucks. Again his natural talents were recognized and he was promoted to Captain and given command of a company.

In 1941, the Ox and Bucks was one of several infantry regiments that began to convert to an airborne role and Howard volunteered for this new and challenging task, accepting demotion to Lieutenant to ensure that he was given command of a platoon. He was subsequently promoted to Major in May 1942.

During the planning for the D-Day landings, MajGen Richard 'Windy' Gale, commanding 6th Airborne Division, had decided on a glider-borne *coup de main* operation to capture the Bénouville and Ranville bridges. He contacted Brig Hugh Kindersley to ask for his opinion on the best company to carry out this task. Kindersley recommended Howard's company. To test the choice, the division was sent out on a three-day exercise in which D Company's role was to seize three bridges from a small group of paratroopers who were defending them. Gen Gale, along with brigadiers Hugh Kindersley and Nigel Poett, followed the exercise and was impressed by the speed and style with which D Company went about their task. Shortly after the exercise, LtCol Michael Roberts invited Howard into his office and told him that D Company would spearhead the British invasion effort and would be charged with capturing two bridges intact. On Gale's orders, the four platoons of D Company were reinforced with two extra platoons. Howard was allowed to select the additional two platoons from any in the battalion and chose two from B Company commanded by lieutenants Dennis Fox and Richard 'Sandy' Smith.

FM Montgomery with MajGen Richard 'Windy' Gale (centre), commanding 6th Airborne Division, and Brig Nigel Poett, commanding 5 Para Brigade (right). Poett would parachute into Normandy and Gale arrive aboard glider Chalk 70. Both men reached Pegasus Bridge by 0900hrs on D-Day. (IWM B7053)

THE PLAN

The planners had estimated that four platoons would be sufficient to capture the two bridges – two to each bridge; but an extra platoon was added for each bridge as an insurance against casualties or the loss of a glider. This would prove to be a wise decision. Howard identified two possible landing zones for the gliders and they were codenamed LZ-X and LZ-Y. To the east, LZ-Y was a long four-sided field bordering the River Orne to the north of the bridge. LZ-X, to the south of the Caen Canal bridge, was the more hazardous of the two landing zones. There was a line of trees to the west bordering the canal, while to the east was a swampy pond, of which they were, however, unaware. The landing zone was triangular, tapering to a point by the bridge.

Howard had decided on these landing zones so that his force would land between the river and the canal, thus ensuring that if one of the bridges was blown soon after the landing, the platoons would not be stranded on the far bank. He also decided to make each glider load a self-contained formation – it would have both engineers and soldiers on board. The crew of a single glider could therefore capture and hold a bridge while the Sappers neutralized the charges.

As he began his planning, Howard was kept up to date with a full range of the latest reconnaissance photographs. In early May, GFM Erwin Rommel visited the two bridges and instructed that the Tobruk anti-tank-gun emplacement should be built and protected by barbed wire and a bunker. Within forty-eight hours RAF reconnaissance sorties had detected this work, and a week later the French Resistance passed on an accurate description. A scale model, measuring 12ft by 12ft, was made to show the bridge in perfect detail, including every building, tree and ditch. The Germans made alterations to their defences almost daily but, thanks to the RAF photo-reconnaissance sorties that took place each morning, the model was updated accordingly.

Key to the capture of Bénouville Bridge was neutralizing the bunker on the right bank of the canal. Three men from the lead section of 25 Platoon, in the first glider to land, would throw grenades through its embrasures. The rest of the platoon were to rush across the bridge and seize the western end. Close behind them, 24 Platoon would clear the remaining positions on the right bank, whilst the men of 14 Platoon, in the last glider to land, would cross to the western side to reinforce 25 Platoon. Exactly the same procedure was to be adopted for Ranville Bridge, with 22 Platoon rushing the defences and taking the eastern end, 23 Platoon clearing the western end, and then when 17 Platoon landed it would consolidate the defences.

The relief would come from the men of 7th Battalion, 5th Parachute Brigade, 6th Airborne Division. They would land in drop zones between the River Orne and the

The 1:1 scale reconstruction of a Horsa glider at Memorial Pegasus Museum close to Pegasus Bridge. The broad black and white D-Day stripes were an Allied identification sign while the black underside serves as camouflage at night. The vulnerable cockpit can be seen clearly. (WF)

Maj John Howard, inspirational leader, shrewd tactician and the man who made possible the remarkable victory at Pegasus Bridge.

River Dives at 0050hrs. Brig Poett, commanding 5th Para Brigade, told Howard that he could expect organized reinforcements within two hours of touchdown. The Paras would come down through the village of Ranville, where Poett would establish his headquarters for the defence of the bridges.

When he was assigned this critical mission, Howard set in place a tough and realistic training regime. He was satisfied with the company, in terms both of its officers and its men, and he also felt at home with them, as many were easy-going but confident young Londoners. In training, Howard demanded nothing less than first-class standards of fitness. He also took his responsibility as a commander very seriously – so much so that for the most part he abstained from drinking in order to keep a clear mind.

There were three weeks of intensive training for the battalion at Ilfracombe in Devon, at the end of which the men marched back to Bulford Camp on Salisbury Plain, a distance of 131 miles. They were carrying 80lbs of weapons and equipment and took only four days to complete the march, though, as Raymond 'Tich' Raynor recalled: 'Some of the lads needed help on the way so we took their packs and carried those as well.' Lt Henry Sweeney, universally known as 'Todd', commanding 23 Platoon, recalled the 'Great March', which took place in two days of pouring rain and two of blistering heat: 'In spite of the toughness and the blisters of it all, we got down to the barracks and we all started singing. Of course the Commanding Officer had come out and you had to march to attention – 140 paces to the minute, which was a terrible pain on your feet. Maj Howard insisted that an officer didn't go back to his quarters and take his boots off until he had ensured that all his men's feet had been inspected, so that any men who had really bad blisters were sent off to the medical inspection room. Then, and only then, were you allowed to hobble away to your own quarters, where you found the food was terrible and the water cold. This was drilled into us – you had to look after your men to the exclusion of everything else.' It was the company's performance on the 'Great March' that clinched its role as the *coup de main* force for the bridges.

Street fighting tactics were taught in bombed-out and evacuated parts of British cities and the men also learned the skills of unarmed combat. Essentially, Howard was taking men from an ordinary British infantry regiment and with good training quietly turning them into special forces.

To make their training more realistic, Howard asked that an area be found somewhere in Britain where conditions similar to those in Normandy existed, in other words two bridges running across a river and a canal with a very short distance between them. Such a spot was found south of Exeter, where the A38 crosses the River Exe and the Exeter Canal at Countess Wear. Howard moved his men down to Devon, where they practised attacks day and night for almost a week. All of this was carried out under the eyes of many curious onlookers from the surrounding area, some of whom interfered with proceedings. One local resident was angry that several tiles had been blown off his roof by an exploding grenade, and the town council felt that the exercises were weakening the bridges, and also they did not like the soldiers fishing with No. 36 grenades. Among the audience for the night attacks was the younger sister of Lt 'Sandy' Smith. She and other youngsters had been evacuated from London and now lived in a large house that overlooked the river. Smith recalled: 'The girls used to lean out of their windows in their nightdresses and watch us throwing bombs and things at the bridge and attacking it. I had to confess to Maj Howard, "Look, there is my sister!" He looked a bit dumbfounded. They told me to keep my trap shut. I told my mother and sister that we were just playing games.'

Howard prepared his men for every conceivable eventuality that they might encounter on the ground, for example only one of the gliders reaching the bridges, or others falling short. In case all the Sappers in the *coup de main* force became casualties, Howard made his men fully familiar with locating and neutralizing demolition charges. They even learned how to handle assault boats, to be used if either of the bridges was blown.

Pte Billy Gray, a Bren gunner in 25 Platoon, recalled: 'We knew exactly what we had to do. We trained and practised it so often that we knew it like the back of our hand. Anyone could have taken each other's place. Each individual soldier knew exactly what he was supposed to do on the night. Lt Fox explained all the eventualities that were covered – "in case none of us arrived, in case one of us arrived, in case one of us arrived in the wrong place or at the wrong bridge, in case we had to carry boats from one bridge to the other". I don't think there was an incident that could have happened that we hadn't rehearsed in one way or another.'

In early May, Brig Nigel Poett assured Howard that he could have anything that he wanted; all he had to do was ask. One notable thing he requested was 'German' opposition for their exercises, in the sense that his opponents should be dressed as Germans, carry German weapons, and should even speak German. All of this was arranged, and the men of the *coup de main* force made a thorough study of German weapons and became familiar with their use. Besides Howard, no one in the company had any idea why they were constantly working on the art of capturing bridges and some were becoming very bored by it. Howard took the men into his confidence and assured them: 'We are training for some special purpose. You'll find a lot of the training that we are doing, this capturing of things like bridges, is connected with that special purpose. If any of you mention the word "bridges" outside our training hours and I get to know about it, you'll be for the high jump and your feet won't touch the ground before you are RTU [returned to unit].'

To Pte Wally Parr of 25 Platoon, the Company Commander seemed to be 'a mad bastard; he'll get us killed one day. Slog! Slog! Slog! Look at C Company; they're not doing it. Look at A Company; they're not doing it. They don't get it – we get it all.'

Lt David Wood, commanding 24 Platoon, recalled that 'It became the talking point of the battalion that D Company did everything rather harder than anybody else. We were that kind of company. We flogged ourselves. He flogged himself – Maj Howard – he didn't spare himself at all but he expected us to do the same. The whole approach was that you were going to do better than the chap next door, even though he was one of your brother platoon commanders.'

In May 1944, the 6th Airborne Division mounted a pre-invasion exercise named Exercise *Mush*. Howard's *coup de main* force were ordered to capture a bridge across the Thames at Lechlade in Gloucestershire. The bridge was held by men of the 1st Polish Parachute Brigade. Gliders were not used to land the company; instead, the men were driven to the general area of the bridge in trucks (since the war many soldiers will have had similar experiences where trucks have become 'helicopters'). The men of the Ox and Bucks then marched to a point within yards of the bridge that represented the landing zones where their gliders would have touched down, and they lay low until a signal was given to indicate that they had 'landed'. The signal was given and Howard's men with their supporting Sappers moved silently forward to the bridge. An umpire was

A soldier of the Oxfordshire and Buckinghamshire Light Infantry dressed in a camouflaged Denison smock over a khaki serge battledress jacket and trousers. His 37 Pattern webbing is light khaki and consists of belt, cross braces, two ammunition pouches, bayonet and water bottle. He has a toggle rope around his waist. He wears a steel rimless helmet with netting cover and scrim garnishing to break up the outline. Around his neck is a camouflaged netting face veil. His face and hands are covered in black camouflage paint. His personal weapon is the Sten Mk V SMG.

Pte Frank Gardner, Capt Brian Priday and LCpl B. Lambley after 22 Platoon had rejoined D Company Ox and Bucks. Gardner has a Bren gun and pistol, Priday a Sten Mk V, and both he and Lambley have toggle ropes around their waists. (IWM B5586)

present on the ground and, although the company had captured their objective, he ruled that they had not and that the bridge had been blown. As was to be expected, the Poles provided a spirited 'enemy'. Lt Hooper of 22 Platoon argued furiously with the umpire over this point, but to no avail. More seriously, in the darkness there was a 'blue on blue' (friendly fire) contact between two platoons and according to the umpires they had inflicted heavy casualties on one another. The role of the *coup de main* force in *Mush* ended in failure. However, there had been valuable lessons for Howard and his men about the tactics required to capture a bridge. It was perhaps the experience of the 'blue on blue' that led to the adoption of the platoon radio call-signs as a simple form of identification – on the night of the attack the men would shout the phonetic alphabet letter that identified their platoon – 'Able' or 'Baker' for example. Happily for Lt Fox's platoon, their identifying shout would be 'Fox'.

At the end of May, the company climbed into its trucks and prepared to leave the battalion camp at Bulford. The rest of the regiment turned out to watch them leave, for, as Lt Sweeney, commanding 23 Platoon, recalled: 'they knew we were going on some special operation. They didn't know what. It was very unusual to see people poking their heads out of windows and coming to the doors of barrack blocks to see you motoring around the square and out. They obviously thought, "We're not going to see that lot again," and off we went.'

The company moved to a sealed camp; its barbed wire perimeter was guarded by Military Police, and from then on the men were cut off from any communication with the outside world. Inside this secure compound, like thousands of other troops destined to land on D-Day, they were told of their destination and learned the reason behind the intense training they had been through in the preceding months.

Sweeney recalled: 'We entered the briefing room one morning and everything was covered up. Maj Howard said to us, "OK, we'll have a little bet. Everybody will put 5 shillings [the equivalent of about £8 today] into the hat and whoever guesses where we are going to land gets the lot." He said, "Alright, now, where are we going to land?" At that stage most people thought that the landing would take place across the narrowest strip – the Pas de Calais – and that finally we had to invade Germany. So I said somewhere in the Antwerp Scheldt area; someone else said the Pas de Calais

MAY 1944

Exercise *Mush* carried out to train the 6th Airborne Division.

BIGOT NEPTUNE

TOP SECRET
Copy No 1
2nd May, 1944
5 PAR BDE OO No 1 Appx A
Ref Maps. 1/50,000 Sheets 7/F1, 7/F2
        1/25,000 Sheet No.40/16NW
To: Maj R.J. HOWARD, 2 OXF BUCKS

INFM
1. Enemy
(a) Static def in area of ops.
Garrison of the two brs at BENOUVILLE 098748 and RANVILLE 104746 consists of about 50 men, armed with four LAA guns, probably 80mm. Four to six LMG, one AA MG and possibly two A.Tk guns of less than 50 cm cal. A concrete shelter is under constr, and the br will have been prepared for demolition. See ph enlargement A21.

(b) Mobile res in area of ops.
One bn of 736 GR is in the area LEBISEY 0471– BIEVILLE 0647 with probably 8 to 12 tks under comd. This bn is either wholly or partially carried in MT and will have at least one coy standing by as an anti-airtps picket.

Bn HQ of the RIGHT coastal bn of 736 GR is in the area 065772. At least one pl will be available in this area as a fighting patrol, ready to move out at once to seek infm.

(c) State of Alertness.
The large-scale preparations necessary for the invasion of the Continent, the suitability of moon and tide will combine to produce a high state of alertness in the GERMAN def. The br grn may be standing to, and charges will have been laid in the demolition chambers.

(d) Detailed infm on enemy def and res is available on demand from Div Int Summaries, air phs and models.

2. Own Tps
(a) 5 Para Bde drops immediately NE of RANVILLE at 'H' minus 4 hrs 30 mins, and moves forthwith to take up defn posn round the two brs

(b) 3 Para Bde drops at 'H' minus 4 hrs 30 mins and is denying to the enemy the high wooded ground SOUTH of LE MESNIL 1472

(c) 6 Airldg Bde is ldg NE of RANVILLE and WEST of BENOUVILLE at about 'H' plus 12 hrs, and moves thence to a def posn in the area of STE HONORINE LA CHARDONNERETTE 0971 – ESCOVILLE 1271

(d) 3 Br Div is ldg WEST or OUISTREHAM 1079 at 'H' hr with objective CAEN.

3. Ground
See available maps, air ph and models.

INTENTION
4. Your task is to seize intact the brs over R. Orne and canal at BENOUVILLE 098748 and RANVILLE 104746, and to hold them until relief by 7 Para Bn. If brs are blown you will est personnel ferries over both water obstacles as soon as possible.

METHOD
5. Composition of Force
(a) Cmd Maj RJ HOWARD, 2 OXF BUCKS

(b) Tps: 'D' Coy 2 OXF BUCKS less sp Brens and 3" M dets.
Two pls 'B' Coy 2 OXF BUCKS
Det of 20 Sprs 249 Fd Coy (Airborne)
Det 1 Wing Glider P Regt

6. Flight Plan
(a) HORSA gliders available 6

(b) LZ-X triangular fd 099745. 3 gliders
LZ-Y, rectangular fd 104747. 3 gliders

(c) Timing. First ldg 'H' minus 5 hrs

7. Gen Outline
(a) The capture of the brs will be a *coup de main* op depending largely on surprise, speed and dash for success.

(b) Provided the bulk of your force lands safely, you should have little difficulty in overcoming the known opposition on the br.

(c) Your difficulties will arise in holding off an enemy counter-attack on the br until you are relieved.

8. Possible Enemy Counter-Attack
(a) You must expect a counter-attack any time after 'H' minus 4 hrs.

(b) This attack may take the form of a Battle gp consisting of one coy inf in lorries, up to 8 tks and one or two guns mounted on lorries, or it may be lorried inf coy alone, or inf on foot.

(c) The most likely line of approach for this force is down one of the rds leading from WEST or SW, but a cross-country route cannot be ignored.

9. Org of Def Posn

It is vital that the crossing places be held, and to do this you will secure a close brhead on the WEST bank, in addition to guarding the brs. The immediate def of the brs and of the WEST bank of the canal must be held at all costs.

10. Patrolling

(a) You will harass and delay the deployment of the enemy counter-attack forces of 736 GR by offensive patrols covering all rd approaches from the WEST. Patrols will remain mobile and offensive.

(b) Up to one-third of your effective force may be used in this role. The remaining two-thirds will be used for static def and immediate counter-attack.

11. Emp of RE

(a) You will give to your Sprs the following tasks only, in order of priority:–
Neutralizing the demolition mechanisms
Removing charges from demolition chambers
Establishing personnel ferries

(b) In your detailed planning of the op you will consult with CRE or RE comd nominated by him in the carrying out of these tasks by the RE personnel under your comd.

12. Relief

I estimate that your relief will NOT be completed until 'H' minus 3 hrs, ie, two hours after your first ldg. One coy 7 Para Bn will, however, be dispatched to your assistance with the utmost possible speed after the ldg of the Bn. They should reach your posn by 'H' minus 3 hrs 30 minutes, and will come under your comd until arrival of OC 7 Para Bn as in para 13 (b).

INTERCOMN

13 (a) You will arrange for an offr or senior NCO to meet CO of 7 Para Bn near their BN RV at 'H' minus 4 hrs 30 minutes with the following infm:–
(i) Are brs securely held?
(ii) Are brs intact?
(iii) Are you in contact with enemy, and if so where, and in what strength?
(iv) If brs blown, state of ferries?
(v) Where is your coy HQ?

In addition you will give your prearranged signal for the brs, to show that they are in your possession, about 'H' minus 4 hrs 15 minutes.

(b) OC 7 Para Bn will take over comd of the brhead and of your force on his arrival at the EAST br.

MISC

14. Glider Loads

(a) Outline.
Gliders 1–4. One rifle pl less handcart. 5 Sprs
Gliders 5–6. One rifle pl less handcart. 5 men
Coy HQ

(b) Detailed Load Tables will be worked out by you in conjunc with the RE and Bde Loading Officer.

15. Trg

The trg of your force will be regarded as a first priority matter. Demands for special stores and trg facilities will be sent through your Bn HQ to HQ 6 Airldg Bde. Until further notice all orders and instrs to you will either originate from or pass through HQ 6 Airldg Bde.

Both Bde HQ will give you every possible help.

APO ENGLAND

(Signed) J.H.N. Poett, Brig. Cmd, 5 Para Bde

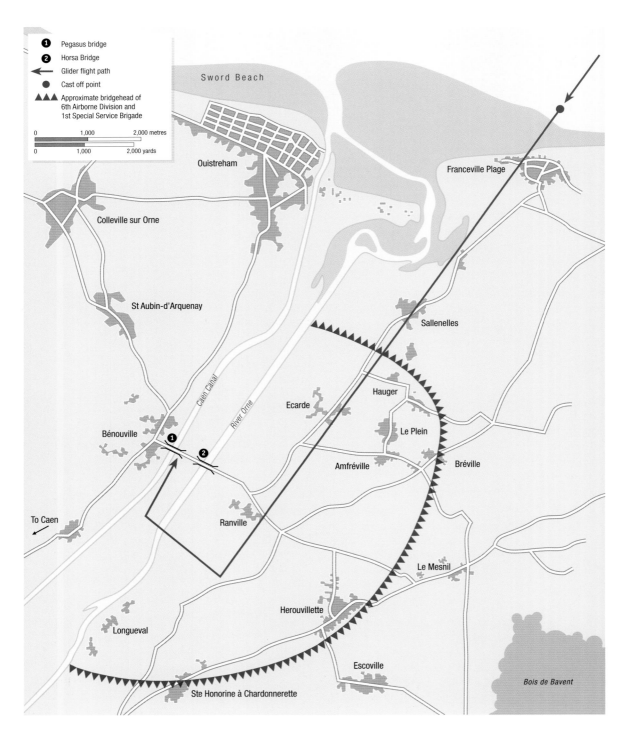

The cast-off point for the gliders was just short of the French coast, but there were few visual navigation aids for the pilots since low cloud cover obscured major features. Flying was consequently done by dead reckoning and timing. There were two critical turns to starboard for the pilots, the first to the south of Ranville and the second over the River Orne. This would place them flying north-east towards their landing zones. However, it was only when the clouds had cleared that they could be certain that they were correctly positioned to land – and then they had to fight as infantry alongside the soldiers of the Ox and Bucks.

and Le Havre. Two people said the Cherbourg peninsula without necessarily knowing there were any rivers.' As winners, they pocketed the equivalent of about £15.

It was a dramatic moment, therefore, when Howard gave the order 'Strip off the paper' and maps, aerial photographs and the superb model were revealed. 'Maj Howard then went through his plan again: how we were going to land and what we would do. After you had been briefed,' recalled Sweeney, 'you then had an opportunity to bring in your own platoon to do exactly the same thing with them, with the Company Commander listening.'

The mass of detailed intelligence was remarkable. 'I don't think there was a bush we didn't know the height of, a ditch we didn't know the depth of or whether it had any water in. We knew the strength of the enemy, we knew where the nearest Panzers were, we knew what to expect, who was coming behind, how many soldiers and how many anti-glider poles there were and when the last one had been put up or how many new holes had been dug. We knew the name of old Georges Gondrée in the café and that he spoke English.'

Several briefings were held and Howard addressed individual platoons and even sections. He encouraged his men to make use of a hut in which all of the maps and photographs were on display, and asked that they study all before them in detail and then talk amongst themselves about any ideas that they could add to the plan.

Gen Gale spoke to the men at Tarrant Rushton and, in a robust morale-boosting briefing, explained the prospect facing the German garrison of the Atlantic Wall: 'The German today is like the June bride. He knows he is going to get it, but he doesn't know how big it is going to be.'

The glider pilots, who had been practising their skills on carefully demarcated landing zones on the British Army training area on Salisbury Plain, were concerned that their aircraft would be overloaded, and so each of Howard's platoon commanders had to tell two of their men that they would not be going on the operation but would rejoin the company after they had landed. A few days later, it was suggested that the company ought to have a medical officer on board because they were going into action completely alone, and so Capt John Vaughan RAMC was included. This meant that another man had to be left behind, but fortunately a soldier had sprained his ankle in a tough game of football and was excluded.

4 JUNE 1944

0900hrs Maj Howard informed that D-Day was on.

BÉRET DU MAJOR HOWARD PORTÉ LE 6 JUIN 1944.
MAJOR HOWARD'S D.DAY BERET.

Maj John Howard's beret: as he was part of the airborne forces, it is in their distinctive shade of maroon, but as he was an officer in the Oxfordshire and Buckinghamshire Light Infantry, the silver bugle horn has a dark green Light Infantry backing. (WF)

OPERATION *DEADSTICK*

Glider No. 1. Tarrant Rushton Chalk No. 91 (Glider No. 667)	
Pilot	SSgt Wallwork
Co-pilot	SSgt Ainsworth MM
Tug pilot	WgCdr Duder, Halifax of 298 Sqn
No. 25 Platoon D Company, 2 Ox and Bucks	
Lt	Brotheridge
Sgt	Ollis
Cpls	Caine, Webb, Bailey
LCpls	Packwood, Minns
Ptes	Baalam, Bates, Bourlet, Chamberlain, Edwards, Gray, Gardner, O'Donnell, Parr, Tilbury, Watson, White, Windsor, Jackson 08
Maj	Howard
Cpl	Tappenden
Royal Engineers	
Cpl	Watson
Sprs	Danson, Ramsey, Wheeler, Yates

Glider No. 2. Tarrant Rushton Chalk No. 92 (Glider No. 661)	
Pilot	SSgt Boland
Co-pilot	SSgt Hobbs
Tug pilot	WO Berry, Halifax of 298 Sqn
No. 24 Platoon D Company, 2 Ox and Bucks	
Lt	Wood
Sgt	Leather
Cpls	Godbold, Cowperthwaite, Ilsley
LCpls	Roberts, Drew
Ptes	Chatfield, Lewis, Cheesley, Waters, Clark 33, Musty, Dancey, Harman, Warmington, Leonard, Weaver, Radford, Clark 48, Pepperall, Malpas
LCpl	Harris (RAMC)
Royal Engineers	
A/Capt	Neilson
Sprs	Conley, Lockhart, Shorey, Wilkinson

Glider No. 3. Tarrant Rushton Chalk No. 93 (Glider No. 663)	
Pilot	SSgt Barkway
Co-pilot	SSgt Boyle
Tug pilot	WO Herman, Halifax of 644 Sqn
No. 14 Platoon B Company, 2 Ox and Bucks	
Lt	Smith
Sgt	Harrison
Cpls	Higgs, Evans, Aris
LCpls	Madge, Cohen, Greenhalgh
Ptes	Wilson, Hook, Stewart, Keane, Noble, Crocker, Basham, Watts, Anton, Tibbs, Slade, Burns, Turner, Golden
Capt	Vaughan (RAMC)
Royal Engineers	
LCpl	Waring
Sprs	Clarke, Fleming, Greenhalgh, Preece

Glider No. 4. Tarrant Rushton Chalk No. 94 (Glider No. 662)	
Pilot	SSgt Lawrence
Co-pilot	SSgt Shorter
Tug pilot	FgOff Clapperton, Halifax of 644 Sqn
No. 22 Platoon D Company, 2 Ox and Bucks	
Lt	Hooper
Sgt	Barwick
Cpls	Goodsir, Bateman
LSgt	Raynor
LCpls	Ambrose, Hunt
Ptes	Allwood, Wilson, Hedges, Everett, St Clair, Waite, Clive, Timms, Whitford, Johnson, Lathbury, Griffiths, Hammond, Gardner 08, Jeffrey
Capt	Priday
Royal Engineers	
LSgt	Brown
Sprs	Deighan, Guest, Paget, Roberts

Glider No. 5. Tarrant Rushton Chalk No. 95 (Glider No. 660)	
Pilot	SSgt Pearson
Co-pilot	SSgt Guthrie
Tug pilot	WO Bain, Halifax of 298 Sqn
No. 23 Platoon D Company, 2 Ox and Bucks	
Lt	Sweeney
Sgt	Gooch
Cpls	Murton, Howard, Jennings
LCpls	Porter, Stacey
Ptes	Allen, Bowden, Buller, Bright, Bleach, Clark 46, Galbraith, Jackson 59, Roach, Roberts, Read, Tibbet, Wixon, Wood, Willcocks
Lt	Macdonald (7th Para)
Royal Engineers	
Cpl	Straw
Sprs	Bradford, Carter, Field, Hadlett

Glider No. 6. Tarrant Rushton Chalk No. 96 (Glider No. 664)	
Pilot	SSgt Howard
Co-pilot	SSgt Baacke
Tug pilot	FgOff Archibald, Halifax of 644 Sqn
No. 17 Platoon B Company, 2 Ox and Bucks	
Lt	Fox
Sgt	Thornton
Cpls	Reynolds, Lally, Burne
LCpl	Loveday
Ptes	Jollet, Halbert, Clare, Peverill, Pope, Whitehouse, Whitbread, Lawton, Rudge, O'Shaughnessy, Ennetts, Summersby, Woods, Wyatt, Ward, Starr
LCpl	Lawson (RAMC)
Royal Engineers	
WS Lt	Bence
Sprs	Burns, C.W. Larkin, C.H. Larkin, Maxted

This list is based on one prepared by Denis Edwards, who, as Pte Edwards D No. 5391739, served in 25 Platoon D Company Ox and Bucks. Though Lt Macdonald, the liaison officer from 7th Bn The Parachute Regiment, landed at Ranville Bridge, he left soon afterwards to attempt to link up with the men of his battalion who were approaching from the east. In two sources Capt Vaughan, the RAMC doctor, is misleadingly named as Jacob. The spelling of Pte Charlie 'Gus' Gardner in 25 Platoon in some sources is given as 'Gardener'. Where two soldiers of the Ox and Bucks have the same surname, the last two digits of their army number have been added; the two Sappers named Larkin are distinguished by their initials. The name of Pte Clare of 17 Platoon is spelt as 'Claire' in the 5 RGJ Ham and Jam battlefield tour; however, this may have been a confusion with the Pte St Clair of 22 Platoon.

Dr Vaughan would look back over 50 years later and smile as he recalled how he was enrolled in the operation. He was enjoying a drink in the Mess when 'Col McEwan came in and said would we have a drink with him at the bar. He suddenly said to us, "I want a volunteer for a forlorn hope." We thought he was exaggerating and there was a nasty silence but everybody was so scared of this chap that we were more scared of not volunteering and therefore offending him, so everyone said they would like to do it. He said, "Well thank you very much, gentlemen," and left the bar. About ten days later I got a message from him: "Come to the HQ. I want to see you." [He said,] "Well, Vaughan, you wanted some action. You're going to get it now. You're going to be attached to a special force." I was then taken down in his car to the camp, where I was introduced to Maj Howard and his men.'

The constant stream of intelligence kept the soldiers and glider pilots up to date with changes around the bridges. Howard was worried by the increasing appearance

Glider pilot. Like the soldiers on board his Horsa, he wears a Denison smock, battledress trousers, boots and anklets and will have his 37 Pattern webbing equipment stowed ready for use following the landing. What distinguishes him is his pilot's helmet and glider pilot's wings on his smock. Once he had landed, he would be integrated into the platoon order of battle. At Pegasus Bridge the first priority for the pilots was to recover stores and equipment stowed on the glider and bring it to the platoon.

of anti-glider obstacles. These were thick poles or logs driven vertically into the ground and spaced at intervals of 15–40ft. Some were linked to mines fitted with pull switches so that if a glider crashed into the poles this would trigger the mines. Nicknamed *Rommelspargel* ('Rommel's asparagus') by the German troops, these obstacles were supplemented by the flooding of low-lying farmland. The flooding would prove very effective against paratroops, who, heavily laden, would find on landing that they were stuck in the sticky underlying mud – many drowned alone in the darkness of 6 June 1944. While some of the construction of these obstacles and defences was undertaken by German troops, the main burden fell on slave labour or prisoners of war, including Italians who had been taken prisoner after Italy sided with the Allies in 1943.

Howard was concerned when he saw that a regular pattern of holes had appeared around the landing zones that seemed to indicate that anti-glider obstacles would soon be erected. In the finest tradition of pilots – both commercial and military – the glider pilots assured their passengers that all was well and any worries that they had were groundless: the obstacles would not pose a problem. SSgt Geoffrey Barkway summed it up: 'I think that if I aim the glider straight between the posts, I might lose one wing or I'll lose the other, but we'll go straight through and they'll help us to stop.' A fellow pilot, 24-year-old SSgt Jim Wallwork, was just as reassuring to Howard, explaining that since the gliders were constructed from plywood the wings would come off if they hit the posts and this would slow down the Horsa.

At 0900hrs on 4 June 1944, Howard was handed a brown OHMS envelope by a dispatch rider. Opening it, he read the brief message that included the code word 'Cromwell'. It confirmed that D-Day was on. But now the weather closed in and by the afternoon wind and heavy rain were lashing the camp. It was perhaps ironic that the camp cinema was showing the American musical *Stormy Weather*, starring Lena Horne. In the mess tent, Fox watched one of the attached airborne engineers take hold of the tent pole and raise himself parallel to the ground using only the strength of hands and wrists. Despite the fact that the camp was 'closed', Fox and Wood managed to slip out and have a beer and dinner with their girlfriends.

'The morning of the 5th was much brighter and we were informed that it was "on" for that night,' recalled Pte Harry Clark of 24 Platoon. 'The company had a day of rest. Sleep, however, was out of the question; we were all too keyed up. A service was

5 JUNE 1944

2230hrs
Troops board the gliders.

5 JUNE 1944

2259hrs
The first glider takes off.

A PIAT in the Memorial Pegasus Museum. Crude, heavy and short-ranged, the PIAT nevertheless would prove critical in the defence of Bénouville and, as a result, in the fortunes of the men landing at Sword Beach. (WF)

A reconstruction of a Horsa cockpit at the Museum of Army Flying, Middle Wallop, Hampshire. In flight the pilot would not have sported the red beret of the airborne forces but rather the helmet with built-in headphones. Horsas were fitted with big 'barn door' flaps that allowed the pilot to make a steep descent into a small landing zone.

held in the afternoon and very well attended it was. All the company sinners, including myself, were present.'

Lt 'Sandy' Smith wrote a letter home, trying to convince his family not to worry. He was certain that he would not be killed but had a realistic attitude to the chances of the operation: 'Nobody had crash-landed a glider at night before on a load of nasty Germans. It made your mind amazingly clear about many things.' For Barkway, the memories of the day before D-Day sound very familiar to soldiers on current operations: 'I don't think we had time to be fearful; there was never enough time to get ready. You know, last minute things, "wouldn't it be better to do this or that ... let's move that here ... you carry this in your glider, we'll carry this in ours ... is there anything we've forgotten?"'

As they sorted their equipment, some men decided to have their heads shaved – this was not bravado but a precaution against infection if they suffered a head wound.

'That evening', recalled Clark, 'about 8pm [2000hrs] we donned our equipment, loaded our personal weapons and boarded the vehicles which were to transport us to the airfield. When we arrived at Tarrant Rushton dusk was just falling. I was amazed at the large number of people around the 'drome. We drove direct to the Horsas and sat on the grass beside them chatting to the glider pilots. The pilots appeared somewhat dismayed at the weight we were carrying. Some kind soul appeared with a large dixie [cooking pot] of tea; on tasting it, we were highly delighted to detect a good mixture of rum in it. We entered the Horsa at 10.30pm [2230hrs] amid cries of "Good luck!" from various bodies.' Chalk had been acquired and the fuselages of the Horsa gliders were covered with confident graffiti such as 'Adolf, here we come!', while Pte Wally Parr named his 'Lady Irene' after his wife.

The pilots were right to be worried about the weight. They had worked out that each man with his weapons equipment would weigh 240lbs. Clark packed his kit, which consisted of 'four Bren magazines, two bandoleers of .303 ammo, six Mills grenades [No. 36 grenade], two No. 77 phosphorus smoke grenades, two Norwegian stun grenades [probably the No. 69 grenade], a 24 ration pack consisting of cubes of tea, soup, oatmeal, toilet paper, sweets and matches and fuel for the little Tommy cookers, a Hawkins anti-tank grenade – to be laid across the road – and a flotation Mae West with two oxygen cylinders attached'. Those men armed with the Sten sub-machine gun (SMG) had the superior Sten Mk V, probably one of the best SMGs used in World War II. It was well-machined and had a wooden stock, pistol grip and foregrip, and could be fitted with the No. 4 rifle bayonet. It would remain in service with the British Army into the mid-1950s.

'Todd' Sweeney recalled that, in addition to the men, the gliders were loaded with 'boats and inflatable rafts and Bangalore torpedoes, because we thought we would have to blow our way through wire. We had our final meal. It was to be a special non-greasy one. But, of course, we were stuffed with goodies. A little pack with a map in it. Benzedrine tablets, glucose and money – French, German, Dutch and Belgian money – in case we were lost. We had maps of Europe that were imprinted on silk handkerchiefs so that you could stuff them in your pocket, a compass that was sewn on to the fly of your trousers. We had files that we had sewn into our battledress pockets so we could saw our way out of prison.'

It was around 2230hrs when Howard watched as the men prepared to board the gliders. 'It was an amazing sight,' he recalled in his diary. 'The smaller chaps were visibly sagging at the knees under the amount of kit they had to carry.' The platoon commander sat at the front close to the pilots, while the platoon sergeant scrambled in last by the rear door. With wonderful understatement, Clark recalled that 'The atmosphere in the glider was somewhat like a London tube train in the rush hour. We were in good heart. John Howard came along and wished us well. We could all feel the emotion in his voice.' For his part, Howard noted in his diary: 'I am a sentimental man at heart, for which reason I don't think I am a good soldier. I found offering my thanks to these chaps a devil of a job. My voice just wasn't my own.'

'The glider doors were closed. We now sat in a world of our own,' recalled Clark. 'I looked across at Lt Wood and I saw he looked a bit tense because he had got a hell of a lot on his mind that night. He was only a boy like the rest of us. He must have been carrying a lot of responsibility and it was going to be put to the test that night... The first Horsa was airborne at 2259hrs. The second, of which I was a passenger, was up at approximately 2300hrs. The remaining Horsas followed at one-minute intervals... The success of our mission was now in the hands of the tug crews and of the six pairs of glider pilots.'

RAID

Inside the lead glider, Chalk 91, Wally Parr led the 28 men of 25 Platoon in a sing-song. With his powerful voice and strong cockney accent, Parr was belting out 'Abby, Abby, My Boy'. However, Pte Billy Gray was almost silent because after enjoying the tea and rum, all he could think about was that it had worked its way through his system and he was now busting for a pee. Looking back, Gray recalled: 'Everybody started singing. If they could have got up and danced they would have. The vast majority of us were Londoners and they were mostly London songs – "Roll Out the Barrel" and "I'm Forever Blowing Bubbles".' At the rear of the glider, Cpl Jack Bailey sang, but he also worried about the parachute brake he might be required to operate. Horsas had been fitted with a rear hatch from which, in theory, a Bren gunner could engage hostile aircraft pursuing the glider; for *Deadstick* this had been modified to take an arrester parachute to provide, theoretically, a safer, slower descent just before landing.

SSgt Jim Wallwork, the pilot of Chalk 91, anticipated casting off, because in the light of the full moon through the clouds he had glimpsed the surf breaking on the Normandy coastline. Beside him, his co-pilot, SSgt John Ainsworth, was concentrating intensely on his stopwatch. Sitting behind Ainsworth, Howard laughed along with everyone when at the close of the song Parr called out: 'Has the major laid his kit yet?' Howard suffered from airsickness and had vomited on every training flight. On this flight, however, he had not been sick. Like his men, this would be the first time he would be in action, and the prospect had calmed his troubled digestion.

One minute behind Wallwork's glider was Chalk 92, carrying Lt David Wood's 24 Platoon into action, flown by SSgt Oliver Boland, who back at Tarrant Rushton had confidently told Pte Clark: 'You've got no worries. I can land on a sixpence.' Another minute behind it was Chalk 93, with Lt R. 'Sandy' Smith's 14 Platoon. The three gliders in this group were going to cross the coast near Cabourg, well to the east of the mouth of the River Orne.

Glider Chalk 91, which transported 25 Platoon and the company commander. The trees were a potential hazard but, using the 'barn door' flaps, SSgt Wallwork positioned the glider at the apex of the triangular landing zone close to the bridge, which can be seen through the trees on the left. (IWM B5232)

The cluttered LZ-X. In the foreground is Glider Chalk 92 (Lt Wood), in the centre Glider Chalk 93 (Lt Smith), and in the distance Glider Chalk 91 (Lt Brotheridge). Café Gondrée is visible beyond Smith's glider. (IWM B7033)

Parallel to that group, to the west and a few minutes behind, Capt Brian Priday sat with Lt Tony Hooper's 22 Platoon, followed by the gliders carrying Lt H. J. 'Todd' Sweeney and 23 Platoon and Lt Dennis Fox and 17 Platoon. This second group was headed towards the mouth of the Orne. In Fox's glider, the tiny figure of Sgt Charles 'Wagger' Thornton was leading the singing of 'Cow Cow Boogie', with the platoon joining in with the chorus.

In glider Chalk 92, with 24 Platoon, the pilot, SSgt Oliver Boland, who had celebrated his 23rd birthday two weeks earlier, found crossing the Channel an 'enormously emotional' experience, setting off, as he was, 'as the spearhead of the most colossal army ever assembled. I found it difficult to believe because I felt so insignificant.' Aboard the glider the youthful Lt David Wood clutched a canvas bucket, a private purchase by officers for their ablutions in the field, but now filled with primed No. 36 grenades. Howard had wondered if Wood, who had joined the battalion at the age of 19 straight from officer training, was 'a bit too young for the toughies in my company'. In the event Wood would be outstanding. Wounded soon after the operation, he remained in the British Army and after the war rose to the rank of Lieutenant Colonel. He was second-in-command of the 1st Bn The Royal Green Jackets – the descendants of the Ox and Bucks – during the confrontation with Indonesia in the 1960s. The last surviving officer from Operation *Deadstick*, Wood was deeply disappointed when on medical advice he could not join in Project 65, the British Forces charity fund raising and memorial event at Pegasus Bridge in 2009. He died on 16 March 2009.

At 0007hrs, Wallwork released the nylon towline from his tug aircraft as he crossed the coast near Merville. There was a sudden jerk aboard each glider, the singing stopped and the roar of the bombers' engines faded. The silence was broken only by the rush of air over the Horsas' wings. Clark remembered that many men called the Horsa gliders 'silent coffins'. 'You know, it was like being trapped in a floating coffin in space... I think people then began to realize what we were heading

6 JUNE 1944

0016hrs Maj Howard's glider lands.

Pegasus Bridge looking east. It was about here that Lt 'Den' Brotheridge was caught in a fatal burst of fire. The newly erected signs can be seen at either end, with a cruder stencilled tactical sign on the bridge. Café Gondrée stands shuttered on the right, while in the distance the Horsa gliders can be seen. (IWM B7032)

for. We were now faced with a situation, there was no going back.' Clouds covered the moon; Ainsworth used a pocket torch to see his stopwatch, which he had started with the cast-off. The first leg of the flight would be between 6 and 7 miles and would take only 3½ minutes.

Seven minutes into 6 June 1944, D-Day had become a reality.

After casting off the gliders, the Halifax bombers flew on Caen, where they were to bomb the cement factory as a cover for the operation. During the battle for Normandy, Caen would be heavily bombed as British and Canadian forces attempted to break out to the south and east. Among the few buildings to survive undamaged was the cement factory. 'They were great tug pilots,' remarked Wallwork, 'but terrible bombers.'

On the bridge, Pte Vern Bonck, a 22-year-old Pole conscripted into the German Army from the area of west Poland now classified as the Greater German Reich, saluted Pte Romer, who was taking over his guard duty. As Bonck walked away, he encountered another Pole finishing his guard duty, and they decided to spend some time in a popular late-night bar in Bénouville. It seemed as if 6 June 1944 was shaping up to be a quiet and enjoyable night.

On the canal bridge, Romer and his companion paced across the planking. Allied air raids were now so common that they ignored the streams of tracer rising and the crump of exploding shells above Caen. The machine-gun crew dozed in the bunker and the anti-tank-gun Tobruk stand was unmanned.

Now, as the gliders started the final descent run, two soldiers held on to Lt Brotheridge's webbing as he began to open the side door. It was at this critical moment that it stuck, and Howard had to help. Looking down through the now open door, all the two officers could see was cloud.

Wallwork was blind too, unable to see the bridges, not even the river and canal reflecting back the moonlight. He was relying on his co-pilot, John Ainsworth, who was watching his stopwatch, while together they monitored the compass, airspeed indicator and altimeter. Three minutes and 42 seconds into the run, Ainsworth said 'Now!' and Wallwork put the Horsa into a full turn to starboard.

Around and below them it was still clouds and darkness. Wallwork said in quiet desperation, 'I can't see the Bois de Bavent.' This huge area of woodland should have been visible to the pilots on the port side of the glider. 'For God's sake, Jim, it is the biggest place in Normandy. Pay attention,' snapped Ainsworth. 'It's not there,' he replied. 'Well, we are on course anyway,' Ainsworth replied and started counting: 'Five, four, three, two, one, bingo. Right one turn to starboard onto course.' Wallwork pulled on the controls and executed another turn to head north, hopefully along the east bank of the canal. They were descending rapidly and using the big 'barn door' flaps. He brought the glider down from 7,000ft to about 500ft and reduced the airspeed from 160mph to about 110mph.

Behind them the pilots could just glimpse flames, searchlights and tracer fire over Caen. Ahead they could still see nothing.

Their target was a small triangular field, about 500yds long, with the base on the south, and the tip near the south-east end of the canal bridge. Though Wallwork could still not see it, he had studied photographs and the model of the area so long and so hard that he had a vivid mental picture of what he was headed towards. As part of their training, the pilots had studied a film that had been made of the model of the bridge and landing zone – a small cine camera had been attached to a curved wire that replicated the Horsa's downward flight path and so, long before computer-generated imagery and computerized simulation, technology had been employed as a training aid with considerable imagination.

Then suddenly they saw the bridge, with its superstructure and the water tower to the east, and the dominant features of the flat landscape. There was the machine-gun bunker just north of the bridge, on the east side, and the anti-tank-gun Tobruk across the road from it; with the zigzagging trenches linking them, these defences were surrounded by barbed wire.

In the final briefing, Howard had told Wallwork that he wanted the nose of the Horsa to break through the barbed wire. Privately the young Staff Sergeant thought that there was very little chance that he could land the heavily overloaded Horsa glider with such precision, at midnight, over a bumpy and untested landing strip. However, he assured Howard he would do his best. What he and Ainsworth really thought was that such a sudden stop would result in at best 'a broken leg or so, maybe two each', and they agreed that they would be lucky if they escaped with only broken legs.

Along with the constant concern about his location, and the intense effort to penetrate the darkness and clouds, Wallwork had other worries. He would be doing between 90mph and 100mph when he hit the ground. If he hit a tree or an anti-glider pole, he would be dead and the men aboard either injured or stunned and incapable of seizing the bridge. The parachute brake in the back of the glider was an extra worry. He feared that if it was operated it would pitch the nose forward and send the glider into a vertical dive. The control mechanism for the parachute was over Ainsworth's head. At the proper moment, he would press an electric switch and the hatch would fall open, and the parachute brake deploy. When Ainsworth pressed another switch, the parachute would fall away.

At 0014hrs, Wallwork called over his shoulder to Howard to get ready. To prevent deafness as the air pressure changed rapidly in the steep dive to the

The plaque at Pegasus Bridge that commemorates Lt Brotheridge. He was comparatively old for a platoon commander, having been promoted from the ranks. Though he was known formally as 'Mr Brotheridge', the men of his platoon, who had huge respect for their officer, knew him as 'Denny' behind his back. (WF)

Bénouville D-Day 1944

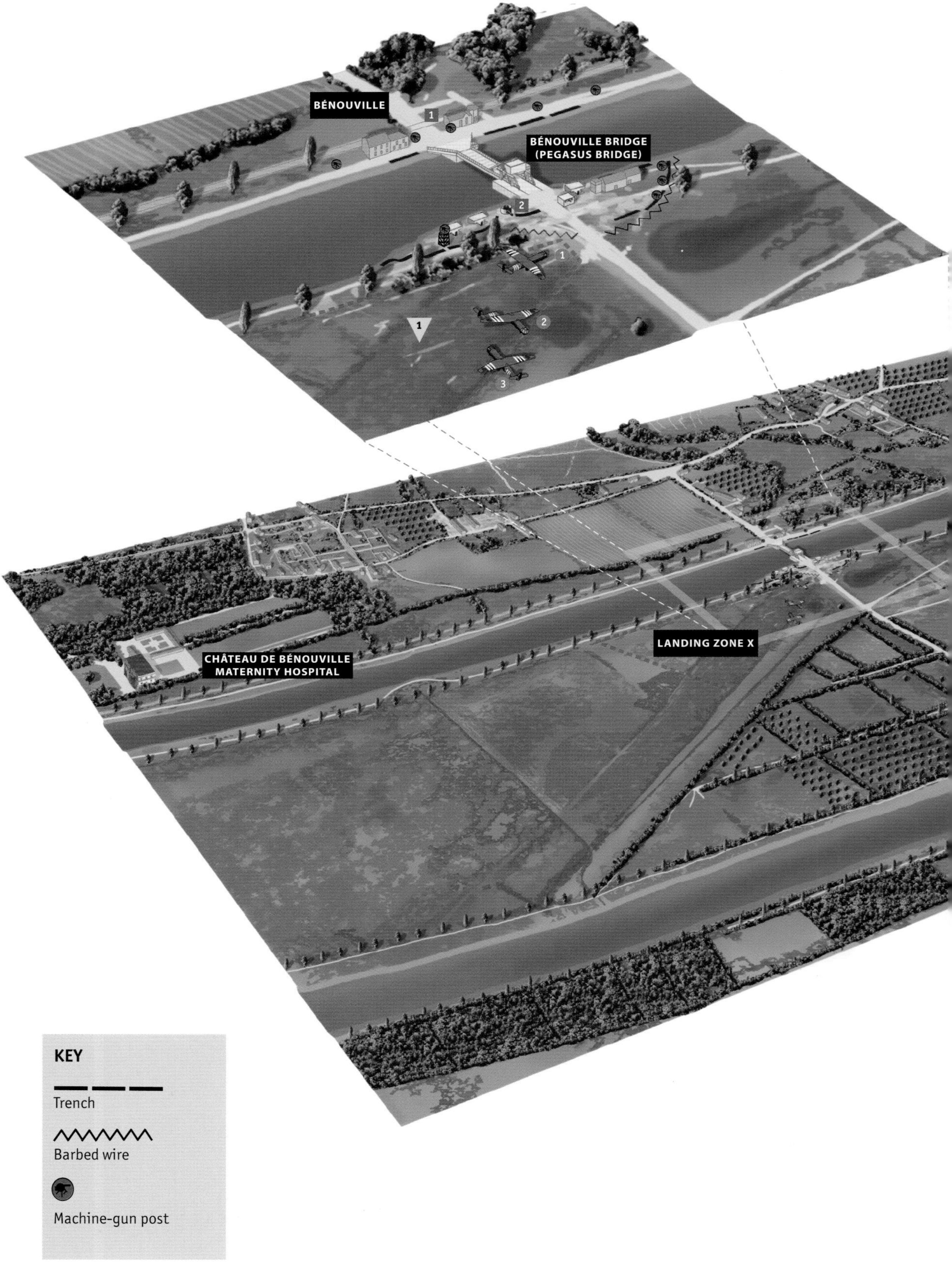

BÉNOUVILLE

BÉNOUVILLE BRIDGE
(PEGASUS BRIDGE)

CHÂTEAU DE BÉNOUVILLE
MATERNITY HOSPITAL

LANDING ZONE X

KEY

Trench

Barbed wire

Machine-gun post

THE CAPTURE OF THE CAEN CANAL AND ORNE BRIDGES

6 JUNE 1944

The two landing zones chosen by Maj John Howard were within the 'island' formed by the Caen Canal and the River Orne, this ensured that his forces were concentrated and if one or both of the bridges were blown, they would not be split up and cut off on the far side of a water obstacle. Though planners in the UK reckoned that each bridge could be captured and held by two platoons, an extra platoon was assigned to the task as a precaution, and on the day this was fully justified. While the square field that had been chosen as LZ-Y was a viable landing zone, the triangular LZ-X was more challenging.

GERMAN FORCES ▮1▮-▮2▮

1 Troops from 736th Gredadier Rgt, 716th Inf Div

2 75mm anti-tank gun

BRITISH FORCES ❶-❺

1 Glider Chalk 91 (Lt Brotheridge, 25 Platoon and Maj Howard

2 Glider Chalk 93 (Lt Smith, 14 Platoon)

3 Glider Chalk 92 (Lt Wood, 24 Platoon)

4 Glider Chalk 96 (Lt Fox, 17 Platoon)

5 Glider Chalk 95 (Lt Sweeney, 23 Platoon

EVENTS ▼

1 0016hrs – Horsa Chalk 91 carrying 25 Platoon lands close to the bridge across the Caen Canal. At 0020hrs Horsa Chalk 92 follows, and finally Chalk 93 lands between the two gliders, dangerously close to the two aircraft and a swampy pond that had not been noticed in the planning. The platoons move across the bridge, secure it, and move into the village of Bénouville.

2 0017 hours – Horsa Chalk 95 hits an air pocket and descends rapidly, landing 1,300 yds from the bridge at Ranville. Vital minutes elapse as they cross the field to reach the objective. At about the same time, Chalk 96 lands closer to the bridge and Lt Fox leads 17 Platoon in a sprint for the objective which is captured without a fight.

3 The ambush of Maj Schmidt's half-track and dispatch rider

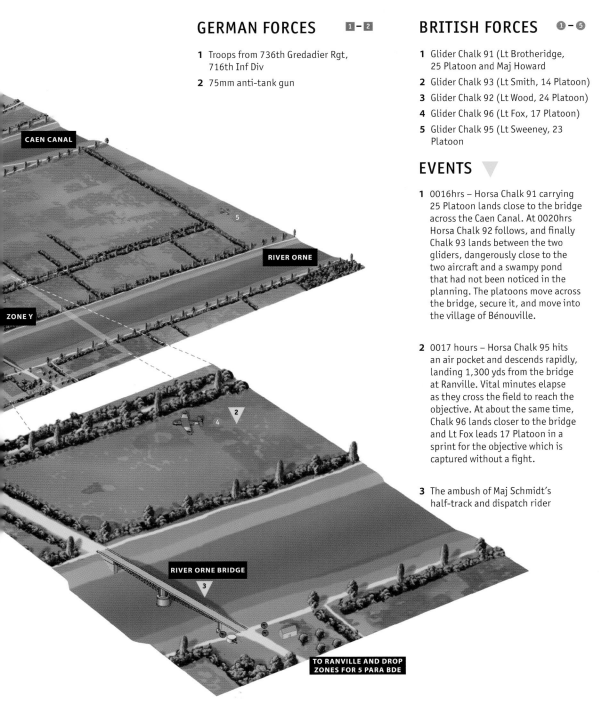

CAEN CANAL

RIVER ORNE

ZONE Y

RIVER ORNE BRIDGE

TO RANVILLE AND DROP ZONES FOR 5 PARA BDE

A high-altitude vertical air-reconnaissance photograph showing the two bridges and the gliders. Glider Chalk 95 carrying 'Todd' Sweeney's platoon can be seen at the extreme left of the photograph – his men had to run the full length of LZ-Y before they reached the bridge, which fortunately had been secured by 17 Platoon. (IWM MH24891)

landing zone, 'We had to shout like hell, we also had to link arms to prevent us from being thrown around inside the glider, and to lift our feet up before landing as it could take your legs off landing at 90mph on rough ground,' recalled 'Tich' Raynor. Howard and the men linked arms and locked their fingers in what was called a 'butcher's grip' and brought their knees up off the floor of the glider. Thoughts like 'No turning back now', 'Here we go' or 'This is it' flashed through all the soldiers' minds. Howard recalled: 'I could see old Jim holding that bloody great machine and driving it in at the last minute. The look on his face was one that one could never forget. I could see those damn great footballs of sweat across his forehead and all over his face.'

Moments later, at 0016hrs, Wallwork landed Horsa Chalk 91, carrying Maj Howard, Lt Brotheridge and 25 Platoon – but it was less of a landing and more of a controlled crash. The glazed nose of the glider was up against the barbed wire fence

The vertical air-reconnaissance photograph of Pegasus Bridge shows how incredibly cramped the landing zone had become when Chalk 93, flown by SSgt Barkway, started its final approach. The glider narrowly missed the unmarked pond but broke up on landing. (Museum of Army Flying)

150ft from the bridge and with the abrupt halt, the two pilots were catapulted from their seats, smashing through the cockpit windscreen. Behind them, the platoon sat stunned for a few seconds. Howard's seatbelt had broken and he had hit his head on the roof, forcing his helmet down over his eyes. When he recovered consciousness, he had the terrifying experience of being sightless and wondered if he was dead or blinded. A quick tug at his helmet rim resolved the problem.

Pte Billy Gray recalled that Brotheridge had the door of the glider open and shouted to a Bren gunner 'Gun out!' The platoon commander checked that the men had cleared the glider and they raced the 30yds to the bridge. Gray, with his Bren gun, 'saw a German on the right-hand side and let rip at him and down he went. Having shot the first German, I still kept firing going over the bridge. At the other side there was a building. It was my job to clear it. At the time I was breaking my neck to go to the toilet. I couldn't do anything about it. I went to the door of the barn and slung a 36 grenade and gave it the rest of the magazine. I went inside but there was nobody in there. Outside and across the other side of the bridge there was a lot of firing going on.'

For Pte Parr of 25 Platoon, tasked with grenading the machine-gun bunker, there was the realization that his mouth was so dry that his tongue had stuck to its roof. 'I couldn't spit sixpence... I had to shout "Come out and fight, you square-headed

PREVIOUS PAGES
Moments after the glider carrying 25 Platoon had landed within yards of the bridge at Bénouville, the men were out and running hard to reach the far bank and secure the bridge. A phosphorous grenade was thrown into the bunker on the right, that had been identified as the firing point for the bridge demolition, ensuring that it was neutralized. The German garrison fired a red warning flare – but too late.

bastards!", then I got air into my lungs. I think I was choking. I was alright when I got on to the bridge. I shouted "Ham and jam!", jumped over the road and went straight to where I had to go. I got the grenade, opened the door and threw the grenade in. I heard somebody scuffle and say something, so I opened the door and sprayed bullets inside.'

A flare was hanging in the sky as Lt Herbert Denham 'Den' Brotheridge dashed across the bridge, leading the men of 25 Platoon. It was on the far side that he crashed to the ground, caught in a fatal burst of machine-gun fire. Many men would die on D-Day but he was the first. Parr remembered that as he reached the café someone shouted 'Where's Denny?', and as he looked around he saw someone lying in the middle of the road. 'I looked at him and went to run on but stopped dead, came back and knelt down. It was Lt Brotheridge. I just knelt down beside him. His eyes were open and his lips were moving; I just looked at him. I couldn't hear what it was. I put my hand behind his head to lift him up; his eyes rolled back – he just choked and lay back. I took my hand away; he had got one right in the back of the neck. My hand was covered in blood. "My God!" I thought, "What a waste." I don't know if it was the bloke himself or all the years of training he had put into the job. It had only lasted twenty or thirty seconds and he was dead.'

Brotheridge's grave is not in the large Commonwealth War Graves cemetery at Ranville but in Ranville churchyard, close to where he was buried immediately after the fighting was over. This tiny Commonwealth War Graves cemetery has a line of 47 headstones along the churchyard wall and includes the grave of an unknown German soldier.

'Apart from the firing going on, a great deal of noise emanated from platoons shouting codenames to identify friends in the dark and there was an unholy babble of "Able-Able-Able", "Baker-Baker-Baker", "Charlie-Charlie-Charlie" and "Sapper-Sapper-Sapper" coming from all directions; on top of automatic fire, tracer and the odd grenade, it was hell let loose and most certainly would have helped any wavering enemy to make a quick decision about quitting,' recalled Howard.

Horsa Chalk 92, piloted by SSgt Oliver Boland, carrying Lt David Wood and 24 Platoon, came in a minute later, landing a few yards away. In the final moments before they landed Pte Harry Clark remembered the command 'Brace for impact!' from his young platoon commander. 'We all linked arms and lifted our feet off the floor... We just waited; we went in at a steep angle. I felt the jerk of the parachute opening. We hit the ground with an almighty thump, rose into the air again and suddenly we came to an abrupt stop.' To Wood, the Horsa seemed to break in half as it landed. 'I was thrown through the side of the glider, which fortunately was made of plywood, and I found myself on the ground complete with my bucket of grenades, none of which had gone off with the impact.'

To Pte Clark it seemed like an eternity from the order to brace before 'we hit Mother Earth with a splintering crash. The very violence of hitting the ground threw us forward, breaking our safety harnesses. I was propelled through the wrecked side of the Horsa to land flat on my back. Several other members of the platoon were in a mass of bodies alongside me, including Lt David Wood, still clutching his canvas bucket of grenades.'

The men quickly began to clear the trenches. 'I found an MG34 intact with a complete belt of ammunition on it which nobody had fired. There was a lot of firing going on and a lot of shouting. We cleared the trenches on the other side very quickly and saw some boxes of ammunition and mines and things but nothing really in the way of strong opposition. On my '38 set I heard the magic words "Ham and Jam" and knew that the operation had been successful.'

Finally, aboard Chalk 93 the youthful Lt 'Sandy' Smith, who had played rugby at Cambridge, felt a tension similar to that before a big game. Looking back, he recalled: 'We were eager, we were fit. And we were totally innocent. I mean, my idea was that everyone was going to be incredibly brave with drums beating and bands playing and I was going to be the bravest among the brave. There was absolutely no doubt at all in my mind that that was going to be the case.'

Aboard the same glider, Capt John Vaughan, who had trained as a paratrooper, had none of Smith's confidence in the cramped confines of the unpowered aircraft. He kept thinking, 'My God, why haven't I got a parachute?'

However, as the glider hit the landing zone 'I knew we were in trouble,' recalled Smith, 'because there was several seconds between that first bounce and then the most amazing, appalling crash and breaking sounds. I went shooting straight past these two pilots and went through the perspex. I went like a bullet and landed in front of the glider.' At the controls of the Horsa, SSgt Geoffrey Barkway had been faced by the prospect of landing on the tiny LZ on which there were already two gliders – incredibly he placed Chalk 93 between them, but as the scar across the ground and the shattered fuselage testified, it was a very heavy landing. What no one realized was that there was an area of swampy water close to the LZ and, tragically, LCpl Greenhalgh, semi-concussed from the landing and burdened with equipment, drowned in the marshy pond. On the Bigot maps prepared for the operation the pond was marked only as a drainage ditch – an oversight given that air-reconnaissance photographs showed marshy ground. As Smith struggled to his feet, groggy from the violent landing, it was one of his section commanders, LCpl Madge, who brought him to his senses with a crisp 'Well, what are we waiting for, Sir?' As he led his depleted force away from the glider, Smith could hear groans from the smashed fuselage. Among the men lying concussed in the wreckage was Capt Vaughan, the young doctor who had thought that parachuting into battle was a great deal safer.

'Sandy' Smith recalled that he did not charge across the bridge but, suffering from an injury to his knee, led his men at the hobble. It was on the far side that he encountered one of the German garrison, who threw a stick grenade at him. A fragment hit him in the wrist. 'I was very lucky. I don't really know what happened. I just felt this smack. I didn't see him throw the stick grenade. I saw him climbing over the wall to get to the other side and I shot him as he was going over – I made certain too. I gave him quite a lot of rounds, firing from the hip – it was very close range. LCpl Madge came up to me and said, "Are you alright, Sir?" I looked at my wrist and then in the moonlight I saw that the whole of my wrist was bare. I thought, "Christ! No more cricket".'

At this juncture, Smith might have been the nemesis of one of the heroes of Pegasus Bridge. 'I then heard a noise above me. Gondrée ... had got out of bed. In the bed was his wife and his 14-year-old daughter. He was crawling on his hands and knees to find out what the bloody hell was going on. He peered over the window ledge; I wasn't messing around, having just had this bloody German, and I just put my Sten gun up and fired. The bullet went over his head, hit the stone roof of his bedroom and then ricocheted down on to the wooden post, into the boards of the bed between them. Gondrée had disappeared.'

Initially, Georges Gondrée had assumed that the crashing aircraft across the canal from his little café were Allied bombers that had been hit by flak and that some sort of firefight had followed as the crew attempted to escape. As 24 Platoon raced towards the bridge, Gondrée saw in the moonlight a German soldier, who may have been young Romer. 'His features were working, his eyes wide with fear. For a moment he did not speak, and I then saw that he was literally struck dumb by terror. At last he stammered out one word, "Parachutists!"'

Prudently, after the encounter with Smith, Gondrée kept the front door closed and took his wife and two daughters to the cellar to wait out the fighting. Husband and wife had seen soldiers who appeared to be wearing black masks moving in the darkness. It was only with the dawn that they noticed that men were digging in their vegetable patch, and Gondrée realised that no orders were being barked out as they would have been with a German working party. They listened intently and Gondrée thought he heard the word 'alright'.

'Presently there were further sounds of knocking,' writes Hilary St George Saunders in the booklet *By Air to Battle*, 'and this time Gondrée opened the door, to be confronted by two men with coal-black faces. He then realized that it was paint, not masks, which they were wearing. They inquired in French whether there were any Germans in the house. He answered "No" and brought them into the bar and thence, with some reluctance on their part, which he overcame with smiles and gestures, to the cellar. For a moment there was silence; then one soldier turned to the other and said, "It's alright, chum." At last I knew they were English and burst into tears. Madame Gondrée and the children at once kissed the soldiers and as a result were immediately covered with black camouflage paint.'

Earlier, when passing the café, Pte Wally Parr recalled that Lt Brotheridge had been moved to one side and 'I looked again, there was a woman there with two children. It was down two steps at the side of the café, so I looked down and I must have been a horrible sight. I'm trying to tell her, "English friends, English friends". These two little kids right in the middle of this shambles. I thought, "I know, a bar of chocolate". I bent down. "English friends. Just stay here. Look chocolate, chocolate," and she just looked blankly back at me.'

The Tobruk housing the 75mm anti-tank gun now has a safety rail around it. The gun is today in poor condition, badly rusted, but still helps to convey an idea of the formidable defences around the bridge that faced the glider-borne soldiers. (WF)

For five-year-old Arlette Gondrée, the younger of the two girls, it was the first chocolate she had ever tasted but there was something vastly more significant than this delicious confectionery. 'It was the most wonderful feeling. I knew right then that the fear was over and we'd be safe and sound. We all rejoiced and Daddy went up and opened the door to the café and as more and more soldiers arrived my father dug up his champagne and distributed it among our liberators. Ever since then we

have kept up the Gondrée tradition of opening champagne for the veterans on the anniversary of D-Day before going with them to pay our respects at the cemetery at Ranville.'

The café would become the Company Clearing Post and Arlette recalled how suddenly the little building was transformed. 'I remember the casualties being brought into the café. The tables had been pushed aside in the main room and the soldiers were laid out there. Some died on the spot. The kitchen was used as a reception area and the dining room as an operating theatre. Two officers operated at the dinner table [Capt Vaughan and the RMO of 7th Bn Parachute Regiment]. My mother was a trained nurse, and all her old skills came back.'

The word filtered round the platoons that over 90 bottles of champagne, hidden from the Germans in 1940, were being uncorked by the Gondrées to celebrate the liberation. In conversation with the author, Howard recalled that during the day many of the men in the vicinity found an excuse to make a short trip to the Company Clearing Post to enjoy the hospitality of the delighted and courageous French couple.

Pitting in the bridge's counterweight bears witness to the violence of the fighting that followed its capture. The 'splash' of holes and the angle of penetration suggest that this was from an exploding mortar round. (WF)

Back at glider Chalk 93, Capt John Vaughan 'found myself lying on the ground in front of the glider with my face in the mud. My corporal was shaking me: "Doctor, Doctor, wake up!" I heard these frightful groans and somehow staggered to my feet outside the glider. I found this chap mixed up in the wreckage but I couldn't get him out to give him a shot of morphia and staggered away. I can hear the groans of the chap even today. I walked away in the direction of the bridge, which was only about 50yds away. I got to the bridge and the first thing I heard was the clatter of the ammunition going off in this tank that had been hit.'

With the benefit of hindsight, in 1995, Lt David Wood felt that he had been premature in reporting that he had cleared houses by the bridge. As he was making his way back to report to Howard, accompanied by his batman and platoon sergeant, all three were hit by a burst of sub-machine-gun fire. 'In my case I was hit in the left leg. I fell to the ground. I couldn't move – in fact I was frightened because obviously the enemy were there and I thought somebody would come along and finish me off. I shouted and before long my medical orderly [LCpl Harris] came along and very quickly gave me an injection of morphine and splinted my leg with a rifle.' The wound would leave his left leg foreshortened by 1½in, and for the rest of his life he would wear built-up shoes.

Howard, with his wireless operator, Cpl Tappenden, had set up a command post inside a trench near the perimeter wire. He had watched 25 Platoon go into action and, as successive gliders landed, their platoon commanders reported to him and moved off to their objectives. Moments later, Howard and Tappenden came under inaccurate fire. The first news that came in was that Brotheridge had been hit. Howard recalled: 'It really shook me, because it was Den and how much of a friend he was, and because my leading platoon was now without an officer. At the top of my mind was the fact that I knew Margaret, his wife, was expecting a baby almost any time.' Now there was more bad news as it emerged that all three of the platoon commanders at Bénouville Bridge had been wounded. If this was not burden enough, Tappenden had heard nothing from the men at Ranville Bridge.

However, just as he saw that the Ox and Bucks had secured Bénouville Bridge, Tappenden tugged Howard's smock and told him that Ranville Bridge had also been captured intact.

The airborne engineers under Capt Jock Neilson had searched the bridges for demolition charges. The German engineers had planned to raise the bridge before they fired the charges, some using the counterweight as a lever to twist and distort the steel girders and make removal and clearance even more difficult. To the amazement of the men from 249 (Airborne) Field Company RE, there were no explosives on the bridge.

At the Orne bridge to the east, Horsa Chalk 95, flown by SSgt Pearson with Lt 'Todd' Sweeney and 23 Platoon, hit an air pocket on its final approach and landed at the far end of the field 1,300yds from the objective. Glider Chalk 96, flown by SSgt Roy Howard with Lt Fox and 17 Platoon, had landed closer to the bridge. Sgt Thornton remembered that as they started the final approach the nose of the glider seemed to be dipping and Howard was struggling to keep the trim correct. He shouted, 'Mr Fox, Sir! Two men from the front to the back – quickly!' and Lt Fox ordered two soldiers to move to the rear and adjust the loading.

As the glider descended, SSgt Howard could see LZ-Y below him. 'We were now at 1,200ft and there below us the canal and river lay like silver, instantly recognizable. Orchards and woods lay as darker patches on a dark and foreign soil. "It's alright now, Fred. I can see where we are," I said. I thought it all looked so exactly like the sand table that I had a strange feeling that I had been there before.'

'It was a marvellous landing,' recalled Dennis Fox. 'The wheels came off, we skidded on our tummy quite a long way and came to a standstill just like that. It was all peace and quiet. We were thinking we should be riddled with bullets. I tried to open the door. I couldn't open the door. I pulled and pulled. Good old Sgt Thornton came up from the back and said, "You just pull it forward, Sir." It just slid up and we jumped out. Tommy Clare, who jumped out behind me, had unfortunately got his Sten on automatic fire, not on the safety, so when he landed his Sten hit the ground and shot a burst of fire straight into the air. Everybody thought we were being fired at. So we made this arrow formation under the wing we had practised and sat in absolute silence.'

With Sweeney's platoon behind them, it was up to Fox to capture the bridge and, on the informal command of 'To hell with it, let's get cracking', they stormed forward. The machine gunner on the far bank opened inaccurate fire and the redoubtable Sgt Thornton put a 2in mortar bomb on the position. 'We all went across yelling "Fox! Fox! Fox!",' recalled the platoon commander. Sgt 'Wagger' Thornton had already set up the 2in mortar and fired two high-explosive bombs that exploded either side of the bridge at the eastern end. This was sufficient to send the machine-gun crew scurrying into the dark – followed by a burst of fire from their abandoned gun, now under new ownership. Soon after they had secured the bridge, Sweeney and 23 Platoon arrived. As they doubled past glider Chalk 96, in the dark it had appeared like a riverside summerhouse. When they arrived at the bridge shouting their identifying code word 'Dog! Dog! Dog!', Sgt Thornton recalled the meeting between the two officers: 'Lt Sweeney turned up and said "What's happening, Fox?" Fox replied, "The exercise went very well, but I can't find no bloody umpires to find out who's killed and who's alive!"'

At 0050hrs the *coup de main* force heard and indeed saw the first lift of the 6th Airborne Division arriving at Ranville. 'We had a first-class view of the division coming in,' noted Howard. 'Searchlights were lighting up the chutes and there was a bit of firing going on and you could see tracer bullets going up into the air as they floated down to the ground. It really was the most awe-inspiring sight. Above all, it meant that we were not alone.'

The radio signal for the capture of the canal bridge was 'Ham' and that for the river 'Jam'. Howard began to transmit the concise but triumphant message 'Ham and jam'. 'As I spoke,' he recalled later, 'I could hardly believe that we had done it.' The operation had been completed in just ten minutes. To inform troops in the area that the bridges had been secured, Howard took his officer's whistle and blasted out the Morse signal for V – V for victory. Years later, he would laugh that in a BBC television programme about the operation, his demonstration of this signal had broken the recording equipment of the sound man. For the paratroops making their way to reinforce the men on the bridges, Howard's whistle became an excellent reference point as well as a reassuring signal that in the early hours of D-Day one operation had gone according to plan. Meanwhile Cpl Tappenden lay by the company radio set and in his broad south London accent continued sending the success signal 'for a solid half an hour, and that was all I repeated – "Ham and jam, ham and jam, ham and jam". In the end I said "Ham and bloody jam!" The reply came back: "Message received and understood."'

Howard decided that the defence of Bénouville was critical since the area to the east would soon be full of British paratroops, and so he concentrated his company around the canal bridge. 22 Platoon, along with the second-in-command, was missing, having landed alongside the bridge at Varaville, 8 miles away. Howard left 23 Platoon at Ranville and sent a runner to order Fox to bring 17 Platoon over. As he issued these orders, two armoured vehicles could be heard approaching from Le Port, but fortunately neither of them turned towards the bridges and both continued south along the road towards Bénouville. With a possible armoured threat, there was an urgent search for the PIATs (Projector Infantry Anti Tank), which were still stowed in the gliders. To their consternation they discovered that on landing most of them had been damaged beyond use. What appeared in the darkness in the wrecked gliders to be the only available PIAT was given to Fox's 17 Platoon. They were to push westwards from the canal bridge and take up positions at the junction of the roads leading from Bénouville to Le Port. Behind them, also on the western side of the canal, were 25 and 14 Platoons, both under the command of the wounded Lt 'Sandy' Smith, while 24 Platoon was east of the canal, along with Company HQ, providing depth for the defences of the Orne bridge.

The PIAT weighed 32lbs and had a reported, but optimistic, maximum rated range of 750yds. According to some wartime manuals, the 3lb high-explosive anti-tank warhead could penetrate about 4in of armour at a 30-degree angle, although this was considered over-optimistic, and 4in at a 90-degree angle was more realistic. Indeed, there seems to be some disagreement between wartime sources on the PIAT's actual performance: earlier British documents often state a figure of about 3in, whereas later post-war documents give the figure of about 4in or more. It was therefore only just sufficient to defeat the frontal armour of older German tanks, and therefore it was advisable that to be effective the PIAT was fired at the side or rear of an armoured vehicle. It was a spigot mortar with the bomb fitting over a spring-loaded spigot – the recoil would recock the weapon and allow another bomb to be loaded into the trough at the muzzle end. However, the PIAT had no back blast and consequently could be fired from inside buildings or confined spaces. At Pegasus Bridge one bomb fired from a PIAT would have a dramatic effect on the course of D-Day.

Lt Dennis Fox recalled his platoon's advance into the unknown: 'Off we went up the road with Sgt Thornton leading this time, not knowing we were into no man's land, because, although we knew the road and we knew which was the Mayor's house and so on, we didn't know what to expect. A window went up on the house on the T-junction and someone called out in French. My reply was something like "*Nous sommes l'armée de liberation*," and we started to take up various positions. I stayed inside the church, protected by the church gateway. Then we heard the sound of tracks coming and I crouched down beside this wall – there was nothing else I could do.'

It was 0200hrs and in the darkness tracked vehicles could be heard approaching. They may have been from the Panzerjäger Company 1 of 21st Panzer Division. It was a rash move by the lead vehicle commander to probe a position unsupported by infantry, but as he moved down the road through Bénouville prior to turning right to the bridge, he was being stalked by Sgt Thornton with a PIAT:

'The PIAT is rubbish; 50yds range only and you must never, never miss. You've had it because by the time you have reloaded and cocked it everything has gone – it is only issued with three rounds. I decided to get about 30yds from the T-junction. I didn't know what was going on and I was shaking like a leaf. Sure enough, three minutes later, this thing appears. You could not see very much. It was moving slowly towards the bridge. For a few seconds they hung around. Although shaking, I took aim and "Bang!" – off it went. The thing exploded. Two minutes later all hell broke loose.'

The damaged World War I memorial outside the mayor's office in Bénouville bears mute testimony to the tough fight for the little community. The white marble plaque at its foot states: 'After being banned for four years, on 11 November 1944 we returned to pay homage to those who died for our country.' (WF)

What the 'thing' was that Sgt Thornton hit remains the subject of conjecture. Stephen Ambrose in *Pegasus Bridge* quotes Thornton as saying it was a 'Mk IV'. The vehicle certainly had a crew of five since Thornton's number two on the PIAT engaged four men who had jumped clear, but the driver was trapped. Discussions on the web have suggested that the tank was an ex-French Char B1 captured in 1940 and overhauled to equip 21st Panzer Division. However, while French armour was used by the division, it was principally the chassis that was converted to an SP role. Moreover the B1 had a crew of four. Pte Eric Woods, who was number two on the PIAT, recalled: 'On the road on the opposite side of the bridge was a junction and from this emerged three French tanks which had been commandeered by the Germans. Sgt Thornton, nicknamed "Wagger", sighted the PIAT and fired, hitting the foremost tank broadside on. It must have been a direct hit on the tank's magazine, for there was an almighty explosion and ammunition continued to explode for more than an hour afterwards. The two remaining tanks quickly retreated from whence they came.'

In *March Past*, Lord Lovat reports: 'The road junction at Bénouville dipped into a hollow; the main road continuing inland ... to Caen. Down on the left, close to houses, lay the turn-table bridge across the Caen Canal. Burning transport smoked ahead. A German half-track, upturned in a ditch, provided some protection for wounded men.' Could 'Wagger' Thornton's 'thing' have been an armed half-track, or, as Dennis Fox suggests, given the intensity of the secondary explosions, an ammunition vehicle?

In the churchyard, Fox had watched the ambush. 'The ammunition tender started to go up. Well, of course, it was a fireworks display and people actually thought that I was involved in some great battle. I was still crouched behind the church wall and it went on and on. You couldn't move very far because a "whizz-bang" went straight past you. Finally, it died down and we heard this man crying out. Pte Clare couldn't stand it any longer and went straight up to the vehicle which was blazing away, found that the driver had got out of the tank and was still conscious. He had lost both feet. Clare – although he was tiny – was an immensely strong fellow, took him back to the first aid post.' Pte Gray remembered the cries of the wounded driver: 'We could see the tank burning and heard the chap who was trapped inside screaming his head off. It didn't do much for morale. The chap's screams were terrible. We just laid there and listened.'

It appears that the first German troops who probed rather hesitantly towards the bridge came from Panzer Pioneer Company 1; as such it is unlikely that they would have been equipped with tanks but they may well have had half-tracks. Moreover, if a half-track was carrying engineer stores like mines or explosives, the resulting explosion would have been much greater than that caused by ammunition 'cooking off' in a tank.

Arguably, the PIAT ambush was one of the more significant actions in the opening hours of D-Day. The Germans assumed that the position was defended by anti-tank guns and were disconcerted by the noise and violence of the secondary explosions. They pulled back and consequently missed the opportunity of overrunning the men holding the bridges, who would have had little to defend themselves with against a concerted armoured counterattack. If the bridges had been recaptured, it would have isolated most of the 6th Airborne Division on the east of the Orne and Caen Canal and left the British 3rd Infantry Division and 27th Armoured Brigade landing at Sword Beach with an exposed and vulnerable left flank. With the road north clear, an armoured thrust could have been launched against Sword Beach – casualties here could then have been as heavy as those on Omaha and the whole D-Day landings severely disrupted.

In the subsequent fighting in Normandy, Thornton was wounded in the hip; after he had recovered, he transferred to the Parachute Regiment and jumped at Arnhem, where he was hit by a sniper in the leg. At the end of the war, in hospital, he learned that he had been awarded the Military Medal. The citation reads:

1. This NCO landed on the bridge during the night before D-day and on capture of the river bridge went unhesitatingly forward to contact the 7th Parachute Battalion.

2. On a patrol to the West of the canal bridge he knocked out and killed the crew of an armoured carrier with a PIAT.

3. During a counterattack on Escoville on 7 June 1944 he led the Company across machine-gun swept field and on arrival in Escoville cleared the houses and streets with such vigour and without regard for personal danger that it encouraged the remainder to put the same spirit into it.

6 JUNE 1944

0050hrs
Coup de main **force observes the arrival of the 6th Airborne Division.**

The original bridge, preserved at the Memorial Pegasus Museum, still bears the marks of the fighting to capture and hold it against German counterattacks. Here a girder has been punched through by a high-velocity projectile. (WF)

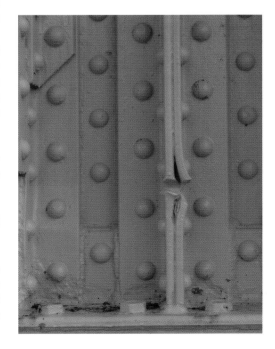

4. At Herouvillette during a heavy shelling and an expected enemy attack he remained on the roof of a shed in order to get better observation and warning of the enemy approach. He remained there until he was seriously wounded in the leg. It was with difficulty that he was persuaded to be evacuated; he considered he was fit enough to continue his observation.

5. This NCO has gained the respect and complete confidence of the men of the Platoon by his enthusiasm, courage, disregard of personal safety and doing his job above the call of duty and with conspicuous gallantry.

However, Lt Tony Hooper and the men of 22 Platoon were not to witness a number of the actions that earned Sgt Thornton his Military Medal and Maj Howard his Distinguished Service Order. Though their glider had come under fire as they started their descent, no one was injured and they touched down perfectly at a bridge at Varaville on the River Dives – 8 miles from their objective of the Ranville Bridge across the Orne.

They deployed from the glider and Hooper left the platoon under command of Capt Priday and set off towards a small copse with two men, to try to orientate the group. Once he had established where they were, he sent the two soldiers back to bring the platoon forward, but, 'It wasn't long before he was making his way back across the bridge accompanied by two German soldiers,' recalled 'Tich' Raynor. 'He had been stripped of his weapon, his map case, helmet and boots.'

The platoon had taken up positions in a ditch adjoining the bridge that he was being marched across and Hooper was talking loudly to alert them. When they were within 10yds, Priday shouted 'Jump Tony!' and Hooper dived away from the Germans. The platoon opened fire at the two Germans but, as one went down, in his death throes his finger closed on the trigger of his MP40 SMG and a burst of fire wounded Raynor in the right arm. In 2009 Raynor joked that he must be the only soldier to have been shot by a dead man. Hooper had been captured because while alone in the wood he had seen a group approaching and assumed that it was his platoon and walked over to them. In a later firefight, Priday's radio operator was killed as the platoon made their way to Ranville, slogging through farmland that had been deliberately flooded by the Germans. Priday recalled: 'For about two hours we swam and waded, going south. In places we had to get non-swimmers across on toggle ropes.' The men found a farm where they were able to rest and sleep in the barn, where their soaked clothing dried out.

'In the morning,' recalled Priday, 'the bombing on the coast whilst the seaborne force came in brought us scrambling for a look. The blast from the heavy explosions shook our rather dilapidated loft until I thought it would collapse.' They set off and en route to Ranville collected members of the Canadian Airborne Battalion, who had dropped in the area, and an RAF pilot.

Meanwhile, on the river bridge 'Todd' Sweeney's platoon were in place and in the darkness an enemy patrol came along the river from the direction of Caen. They were challenged and replies came back in what sounded like German, so the section opened fire. Sadly, the following morning they found that among the dead was a British paratrooper, a Pathfinder who had been captured. Now, as they waited in the darkness, Sweeney's greatest fear was an attack by tanks, since the platoon had only one PIAT.

Then it appeared that his fears had been realized. 'We heard the grinding of gears and the noise of what sounded like a very heavy vehicle coming round the corner approaching from the east. I thought, "Well, here we go. This is the first tank attack," and I got everybody ready. Around the corner came low dim yellow lights and a grinding of gears with the sound of a track running. So I sent a message over the air.

Down the road came an open half-track – an officer's vehicle – followed by a motorcyclist. We were all down in the ditches on the side of the road, and so we were looking up, and as it passed everybody opened fire. To my amazement it sailed straight across the bridge. I was amazed that it went through that hail of fire. I think the driver had been hit because the section on the far side of the bridge saw the vehicle swerving. Cpl Jennings opened fire and threw a grenade in as it went past and the thing slid off the road and into a ditch. This vehicle had gone racing through the Paras' dropping zone heading for the bridge to get there before the Paras could reach it, only to find that we were already there. The officer was still alive. His motorcyclist dropped dead at my feet, swerving across, and was there in the morning.'

A myth has grown up around this action in which Maj Hans Schmidt and his dispatch rider were ambushed on Ranville Bridge. The officer is described as riding in an open-topped Mercedes staff car with the remains of his supper, wine bottles and in some versions even his girlfriend's lingerie. When the young dispatch rider is hit, he flies off his motorcycle into the River Orne. In reality Schmidt was in a half-track, probably an SdKfz 250, with a driver and radio operator, and, while the intense close-range small-arms fire would not have penetrated the ⅛in side armour, the driver appears to have made the fatal error of having the side vision hatches open. Of the young dispatch rider, Sweeney recalled 50 years later that he 'was the first dead body I had ever seen and the realization that we were engaged in a bloody, serious fight suddenly struck home.'

Schmidt had suffered a leg wound and was taken to the Company Clearing Post set up by Capt Vaughan between the two bridges. The RAMC doctor recalled: 'He was an absolute fanatic. He spoke to me in very good English and said, "Your troops are going to be thrown back. My Führer will see to that: you're going to be thrown back into the sea!" – so on and so forth. He wanted me to shoot him. He thought he

Photographed six days after D-Day, the wrecked remains of Glider Chalk 92 have been picked over by the locals for useful items such as the webbing seat harness. The hazardous nature of night glider operations is clearly illustrated by the fact that most of the nose and pilot's position has been smashed. (IWM 7034)

had done a poor job and his Führer will be very upset with him. He cried "Shoot me doctor!" So I got out some more morphia and shot him in the bottom with that, and within twenty minutes he was much more polite and he thanked me for what I had done.'

Sweeney noticed that there was a cottage on the right bank and, as Lt Macdonald moved off to try to link up with 7th Bn The Parachute Regiment, Sweeney crossed the bridge and knocked on the door. It was opened by 'a little old lady and little old man'. In his best French, Sweeney explained that his men had arrived '*pour la libération de la France*', only to have the door closed in his face. Over the years the Germans had conducted anti-invasion exercises with troops playing the part of the Allies, and the elderly couple were clearly taking no chances with these nocturnal visitors. Sweeney would return in daylight, to be greeted with hugs and kisses from the old couple.

From 0300hrs, the first men of the 7th Bn The Parachute Regiment began to trickle in from the drop zone to the east and joined them to thicken up the defences. The battalion had lost all of its signal equipment, machine guns and mortars. Of the 640 men who had taken off from Britain, only 210 had landed safely in France. The loss of the battalion's radios explained why Howard's signaller had initially received no acknowledgement of his increasingly exasperated signal 'Ham and jam'. At this juncture in the action, Pte Harry Clark's section returned to the east bank of the canal and resumed their position in the captured enemy trenches. 'I settled down behind a pillbox and started to get a brew going. It was like nectar and filled me with hope.'

Among the paratroops who landed safely was the Adjutant of 7th Bn The Parachute Regiment, 25-year-old Lt Richard Todd. As they made their way towards the bridges, Todd recalled that he 'knew something was going on because we could hear a certain amount of firing coming from the direction of the bridges. I went along as part of Battalion HQ and got down onto the road that led to the bridges. We realized that the first one had certainly been taken because I could see some Ox and Bucks chaps around there. I then started to run along the causeway between the two bridges. I remember at one point the MO caught up with me, took me by the arm and said, "Can I come with you? I'm not used to this sort of thing." He was rather horrified because we had passed a German who had had his head shot off but his arms and legs were still going and there were strange noises coming from him. I think even the doctor was a bit turned over by that.

'I remember, as we were running along the causeway, thinking "Now we are really going into it", because there was a hell of an explosion and a terrific amount of firing and more explosions – intermittent ones – all the time and tracer going in all directions. It really looked as if there was a real battle going on. It wasn't until we got to the other side and found that it was this tank that had been hit and we realized it was just the ammunition that was exploding.'

Richard Todd, who would enjoy a distinguished career after the war as a stage and film actor, was already established as an actor in the late 1930s. At a pre-D-Day briefing he met the commander of 23 Platoon and they were amused to discover that, with either Todd or Sweeney as their surname, both had been nicknamed after Sweeney Todd, a murderous Fleet Street barber who had a penchant for cutting his victims' throats while he was shaving them – an invention of the 19th-century 'penny dreadful' thrillers. In the 1962 Hollywood blockbuster *The Longest Day*, the account of D-Day based on the book by Cornelius Ryan and produced by Darryl F. Zanuck, it was fitting that Richard Todd played the part of John Howard.

On Ranville Bridge, as the advanced guard of 7th Bn The Parachute Regiment began to double across, Pte Clark's section couldn't resist digs like 'Where the hell

6 JUNE 1944

c.0300hrs Troops from 7th Bn The Parachute Regiment begin to join up with the *coup de main* force.

have you been?' Pte Billy Gray remembered that the Paras were delighted to see that the bridge had been captured, 'because it was their job if we hadn't have taken it to take it. They just went past patting us on our helmets saying "Good lads! Well done!" and away they went. Our particular section was relieved and told to go back to the gun pit where there was a 75mm gun. So we went and took charge of that.'

Today the gun in the Tobruk is still in place at the new Pegasus Bridge. However, much has changed: with the widening of the Caen Canal, the gun was moved, and for the safety of the public a rail is in place around the pit; the trenches, wire and the bunker that housed the firing point for the demolition charges have now gone; so, too, have the bunkers and other field works. However, back in June 1944 the men of 25 Platoon found that there was a labyrinth of tunnels underneath the gun pit. Pte Wally Parr recalled that, equipped with a torch, he began to move carefully through the complex. 'In the first bay there was a bed and some curtains; in the second nothing. When I came to the third, I pulled the curtain back and shone the torch in. There was a blanket there and there was a figure underneath it. We walked in, leaned over and pulled the blanket back. There was a young German in there, shaking from top to toe; he could hardly walk. He was writing a letter. There was a big pad of paper, I picked it up and stuck it in my camouflaged jacket.'

Sgt Thornton and Lt Fox were also working their way through the trenches and bunkers close to Maj Howard's HQ. After the firefight and explosions around the position, Fox 'assumed that they were empty. However, Sgt Thornton, as ever, came up to me and told me that there were three Germans asleep in the trench. It was a very handsome trench; you went down into this deep dugout and you went further down and you came to this well dug-out bunk room with three bunks in it, one on top of the other. He took me down to show me and there were three Germans fast asleep with their rifles neatly stacked in the corner. Sgt Thornton said he would take the rifles before I did anything and then I shook the nearest German. I ripped the blankets off him and shone the torch in his face and said "Komm! Komm!" The German just looked up at me, reached for the blanket and said whatever is the German for "Oh, fuck off!" and went back to sleep. Thornton cried his heart out and lay on the floor laughing his head off.'

Blinded by the torch and addressed in German, the enemy soldier thought it was one of his friends having a joke. 'It never occurred to him that this was the enemy,' said Fox. 'It took the wind right out of my sails. Here was a young officer, first bit of action, first Germans I had seen, giving them an order and being taken no notice of. It was a bit deflating.'

Exasperated, Fox turned to Sgt Thornton and said: 'Blow this for a lark! You take over.' 'I suppose I could have shot them all,' recalled Thornton, 'but I don't believe in murdering people in cold blood, so I put my Sten gun on to automatic and fired it along the bottom of the bunks. They moved like greyhounds.'

Soon after this, Fox would have another encounter with his enemy and find that he was very human. 'Sgt Thornton brought up another German he had found and he wondered if I would like to interrogate him to see if there were any more about. This German ... was only a youngster and he did speak a bit of broken English. I had no German, but funnily enough we both of us spoke a bit of Latin, so we lapsed into Latin with a bit of French. I wanted to know who he was and he said, "What are you doing here? What is going on?" I said we were landing and he was our prisoner. He said "Come off it! Where did you land? We didn't hear you land. Where did you come from?" I explained to him. What it was turning into was me being interrogated. He didn't want to fight, or to be killed. He then produced photographs of his family, which I admired until Sgt Thornton came up and relieved me of him.'

At dawn, the Allied naval bombardment in support of the landings on the beaches began. Howard wrote: 'The barrage coming in was quite terrific. It was as though you could feel the whole ground shaking toward the coast, and this was going on like hell. Soon afterwards it seemed to get nearer. Well, they were obviously lifting the barrage farther inland as our boats and craft came in, and it was very easy, standing there and hearing all this going on and seeing all the smoke over in that direction, to realize what exactly was happening and keeping our fingers crossed for those poor buggers coming by sea. I was very pleased to be where I was, not with the seaborne chaps.'

With first light, German snipers began to target the small force around the bridge. It was a lethal hazard that would trouble them for the rest of the day. Lt Smith had just had his arm bandaged by a medical orderly, who then stood up, 'when one of the snipers shot him straight through the chest – knocked him for miles. He went hurtling across the road and landed on his back, screaming "Take my grenades out! Take my grenades out!" He was frightened the second shot might hit the grenades he was carrying. I remember that was a very low point in my life. I thought that the next bullet was going to come for me. I felt terrible.'

Lt Richard 'Sandy' Smith would be awarded the Military Cross for his part in Operation *Deadstick*. The citation read: 'Although injured in the hand during a crash landing of a glider in the airborne operation at Bénouville Bridge on 6 June 1944, Lieutenant Smith brilliantly led his platoon onto the bridge and successfully cleared several houses and co-ordinated the defence of his platoon. It was only when their duties were finished that he allowed himself to be attended to and was finally evacuated to the Main Dressing Station.'

In the summer heat of June 1944 a section of British soldiers crosses the bridge going west. Just visible on the left, a sandbagged anti-aircraft-gun emplacement has been constructed on the roof of the bridge control tower. (IWM B5290)

More prisoners were brought in by Sgt Thornton – two Italian slave labourers who had cycled up to the bridge to continue their work of erecting anti-glider poles. Howard remembered them as 'miserable little men, in civilian clothes, scantily dressed, very hungry'; regarding them as being completely harmless, he ordered that they be set free and given a 48-hour ration pack. They 'immediately went off toward the LZ, where they proceeded in putting up the poles. You can imagine the laughter that was caused all the way around to see these silly buggers putting up the poles.'

At about 0800hrs, two RAF Spitfires flew low over the bridges to check on their condition, and on Howard's order a ground signal was laid out to show they had been secured. The pilots made several passes and a number of victory rolls, but before they disappeared one of the pilots was seen to drop something from the cockpit. Howard sent a section to investigate and they found that he had dropped a selection of the early editions of that day's newspapers. While there was nothing about D-Day, they provided a most welcome distraction as they were passed around. For the men of the *coup de main* force, Howard told the author, the real interest was the racy cartoon strip in the *Daily Mirror* featuring the adventures of Jane, a scantily clad young lady who in various roles took on the might of the Third Reich, defeating evil agents, arrogant officers and other villains.

At 0900hrs, Howard saw 'the wonderful sight of three tall figures walking down the road. Now, between the bridges you were generally out of line of the snipers, because of the trees along this side of the canal, and these three tall figures came marching down very smartly and they turned out to be Gen Gale, about 6ft 5in, flanked by two 6ft brigadiers – Kindersley on one side, our own Airlanding Brigade commander, and Nigel Poett, commanding 5th Para Brigade, on the other.' Richard Todd said that 'for sheer bravado it was one of the most memorable sights I've ever seen.' Pte Clark recalled: 'We had a visit from Gen Gale and Brig Poett during the morning; we even got a shout of "Good morning, chaps" from them.'

Shortly after, a gunboat approached Bénouville Bridge from the direction of Ouistreham. No crew were visible but the boat was armed with a 'wicked looking' 20mm gun. The craft kept closing and, once it was within range, men of the 7th Battalion opened up with small-arms fire. Cpl Claude Godbold, who, with Lt Wood and Sgt Leather both casualties, was now in command of 24 Platoon, waited until the boat was within 50yds and fired the platoon PIAT. Pte Clark watched the unusual naval action. (The next time an anti-tank weapon would be used against a warship would be in South Georgia in 1982 when 22 Royal Marines under Lt Keith Mills engaged heliborne Argentine forces and an Argentine warship, the ARA *Guerrico*. The ship was hit and crippled by 66mm LAW rockets and an 84mm Carl Gustav round.)

'Much to my amazement,' recalled Clark, 'he hit the boat just behind the wheelhouse. It turned and headed for the bank. Knowing the boat would cover us from snipers, I moved forward and took two prisoners.' The crew might have surrendered willingly but Howard remembered the captain, who was 'an 18- or 19-year-old Nazi, very tall, spoke good English. He was ranting on in English about what a stupid thing it was for us to think of invading the Continent, and when his Führer got to hear about it that we would be driven back into the sea, and making the most insulting remarks, and I had the greatest difficulty stopping my chaps from getting hold and lynching that bastard on the spot.' Howard had him escorted to the POW cage in Ranville for interrogation, 'and he had to be gagged and frog-marched because he was so truculent and shouting away all through the time.' It took a thump on the shoulders from Clark's rifle to silence the German.

6 JUNE 1944

0800hrs
Success signals laid out for RAF Spitfires observing the bridges.

6 JUNE 1944

0900hrs
Gen Gale arrives at the bridges.

British infantry hitch
a ride on a Universal Carrier
across Pegasus Bridge (top).
The walkway is on the left of
the bridge and offered some
cover to men making the
hazardous journey across
it. After the war a new
bridge control tower was
built (bottom), while the
bunker on the right of the
bridge was incorporated into
the cellar of a house. Both
disappeared when the canal
was enlarged. (Private
collection. IWM B5234)

Now, as Clark escorted them towards Ranville Bridge, the German prisoners realized that they too were at risk from their own snipers. 'I took them forward to the bridge. As we were about to cross the bridge I noticed a paratrooper lying on the right-hand side of the road. He was in obvious agony. I went up to him and it was obvious he had been shot through the spine. He asked me to put him out of his agony.' The little party now came under intense sniper fire. 'I said to the two Germans "Run", and I prodded them both with my outstretched rifle to indicate that they should run. By this time they had guessed why and they ran like the devil until we got to the far side of the road when we could get into a dip in the road.'

A second boat approached from the direction of Caen and another anti-tank action ensued, but this time using the gun in the Tobruk. It was Pte Wally Parr of 25 Platoon who turned gunner. His gun team had worked out how to load but were unable to find how to fire until one man spotted a button and pressed it. There was a loud bang and a shell went flying off towards Caen. Having worked out the drills, the approaching patrol boat was an obvious target. They fired one round – and missed. However, at 300yds the second shot found its target and the skipper, not being made of the fanatical stuff of the earlier boat's captain, turned around and made off back towards Caen. The gun crew were now on form and a second round hit the boat as it withdrew.

With snipers becoming an increasing threat, Parr decided that the water tower on the high ground to the west of Bénouville was an obvious observation post for snipers. Two rounds hit the target and there were cheers from the soldiers on the canal as water gushed from the holes punched by the armour-piercing ammunition. Looking south down the canal, he saw the imposing outline of the Château de Bénouville. Howard was startled by Parr's command 'No. 1 gun, fire!', since he was not aware that there was more than one gun in the vicinity. Parr's crew slammed three rounds into the Château's roof. Some months later, reading an American magazine, he came upon a story about Pegasus Bridge that included the fact that the cowardly Germans had shelled the maternity hospital in the Château de Bénouville. Chastened, Parr recalled that 'this was the first and last time I had shelled pregnant women and newborn babies'.

Pegasus Bridge about a week after its capture. Bailey bridge panels are stacked to the left by the truck, probably destined for the bridge across the Orne. The bunker that was the firing point for the bridge demolition can be seen on the right. (IWM B 5296)

The 75mm anti-tank gun that was taken over by Pte Wally Parr and fired on the water tower and the Château de Bénouville, which he only later discovered was a maternity home, whose director had been an active member of the Resistance. (WF)

Not all the soldiers on the canal were happy with Parr's new enthusiasm. Pte Gray remembered that it was 'a blinking nuisance'. 'Every time it started to get quiet, Wally would fire this bloody gun and Jerry would start off again, so we were all onto him, "Don't fire the blinking gun."' After a few more shots, Howard had to restrain him as he felt that some were a little reckless.

At 1000hrs, a fighter-bomber, probably an Fw 190 of JG2 based at Cormeilles-en-Vexin, came roaring down towards the canal bridge and the men dived for cover. Howard sheltered in his pillbox. The aircraft released a bomb that hit the bridge at an angle, failed to explode and bounced off into the canal. 'What a bit of luck that was, and a wonderful shot it was by that German pilot,' noted Howard.

It was an indication of the importance that the German High Command attached to the two bridges that in the days following D-Day they would deploy their limited air resources in an attempt to destroy them. On 9 June at 1425hrs, nine Fw 190s of I. and II./JG1 took the air for an escort mission to 'target area XW4E', followed a minute later by just four machines from the battered III./SG4, whose mission was to attack a bridge over the River Orne. In the face of intense

6 JUNE 1944

1000hrs German fighter-bomber unsuccessfully attacks the canal bridge.

light and medium anti-aircraft fire, they dived from 4,000ft and dropped two SD 500s and an SC 250, claiming two large explosions at the head of the bridge and a direct hit which destroyed it. It was an optimistic and confused report in which the German pilots stated that the Thunderbolts and Mustangs operating in the area had not hindered them – it is unlikely that these American aircraft would have been over the British sector.

Back on 6 June, it was now nearing midday, 'and I was very hungry,' recalled Pte Harry Clark of 24 Platoon. 'I decided to open the 24-hour ration pack; it contained a load of rubbish in the form of soup and oatmeal cubes plus some very hard biscuits. The only items of any use were several cubes of tea, sugar and milk. The remainder was consigned to the Caen Canal. It was fortunate that I had hoarded my chocolate ration for six weeks.'

At 1330hrs, above the explosions and gunfire, some of the paratroops and glider-borne troops thought they heard the distinctive sound of bagpipes. Sweeney nudged Fox as they sheltered together half-asleep and said, 'You know, Dennis, I can hear bagpipes,' and received the reply, 'Don't be stupid, we're in the middle of France, you can't have bagpipes.' The redoubtable 'Wagger' Thornton was similarly sceptical: 'Bagpipes? What are you talking about? You must be bloody nuts.' 'All of a sudden, through the trees came this guy playing the pipes with a green beret on [and] Lord Lovat behind him.' Pte Eric Woods, who was on guard that morning, asked his companion, 'Do the Germans play the bagpipes?' – to which he replied, 'I don't think so.' 'I said that I thought I could hear bagpipes.' Confirmation came a few minutes later. The sounds of the pipes grew louder as the Green Berets of Lord Lovat's force advanced towards Pegasus Bridge.

While the idea of going to war in the mid-20th century with a piper may seem anachronistic, for Lord Lovat, commanding the 1st Special Service Brigade, an elite Commando force, equipped with relatively short-range and unreliable radios, 'Blue Bonnets over the Border' played by his piper, Bill Millin, would be a simple and effective way of alerting the men at the bridge that the Commandos were approaching.

The scene before the Caen Canal was widened, with the original bridge in place. The Tobruk housing the anti-tank gun is on the left, Café Gondrée across the canal, and in the foreground is one of the *Monuments signaux* erected by the Comité du Débarquement at significant D-Day locations. (Private Collection)

6 JUNE 1944

1330hrs Lord Lovat and the 1st Special Service Brigade arrive at the bridges.

Recalling the event 50 years later, 'Todd' Sweeney wrote in the Ox and Bucks regimental journal: 'Along the towpath coming towards us was one lone piper playing merrily away. Some 50yds behind him stretched a long line of troops; the Commandos had arrived to help us. A bugler stood up nearby and sounded a call. Hollywood could not have contrived a more dramatic scene. Those who had landed from the sea had linked up with those who had landed from the air.'

The Commandos had landed at Sword Beach and after a hard fight pushed inland fast. On the way they had been joined by a lone Duplex Drive amphibious Sherman tank of the 13th/18th Hussars, which had given them invaluable support. The Commandos had then captured a German horse-drawn transport unit made up of former Soviet POWs conscripted into the Wehrmacht. The Russians were happy to surrender and the carts were quickly loaded with radios, rucksacks and, at the rear, the spare ammunition. As they approached the now much fought-over T-junction, Lovat noticed 'dead of both sides sprawled about the hollow, where airborne troops dug deeper into slit trenches. Others brewed up tea; the scene reminiscent of some Indian swoop on the wagon train in a western movie.'

Despite fatigue and the strain of the fighting, it was irresistible for the Londoners of the Ox and Bucks, seeing the Commandos with their horse-drawn transport, to break into a chorus of ''Ammer, 'Ammer, 'Ammer down the 'Ard 'Igh Road'. However, the horses and carts were useful for bringing in casualties to the café Company Clearing Post.

Lovat reached the canal bridge, which, as sniper rounds cracked overhead, he recalled as a 'hot potato'. Linking up with Howard, he shook his hand and declared, 'John, today history is being made.' Lovat remembered Howard as 'a modest fellow'. 'I remember an apology as we doubled across this hot potato: "Sorry about the mortaring from that ruddy château. The bastards have got the range, but it happens

The *pont tournant* across the Orne. Visible top left, was a single-lane bridge and consequently, as the traffic increased, a pontoon Bailey bridge was constructed upstream. Here Sappers are rafting across a section of the bridge. Today, the footings for this bridge are still visible at low tide. (IWM B5231)

to be a maternity hospital and I have strict orders not to disturb the inmates."'
To Lovat the countryman, the meadows between the bridges 'provided a nasty spectacle: swollen cattle and horses lay with legs in the air, while others dragged around, tripping on spilled insides, bellowing their agony. Two Schmeisser men under Sgt Phillot ran over to put them out of pain.'

The snipers around the bridge would take a terrible toll of the Commandos. For Dennis Fox, the site would haunt him: 'Lovat's men were trying to cross this bridge and being shot at by this sniper. There was a waste. One after another, these young chaps just crumpled. You didn't hear the shot, you just saw them crumple. These chaps with great big packs, loaded up, had marched inland and were jolly tired. Every now and then a man would fall and more and more fell. The others just carried on, they were so tired. I think they felt "If we're going to be sniped then we're going to be sniped" sort of thing.'

Among the Commandos who died on the bridge was LCpl Mullen, a gifted artist. Lord Lovat would write of him: 'Wounded and half-drowned in the landing, pulled over by a heavy rucksack, then picked out and dragged over the sand, Mullen the artist, like a broken doll, lay with both legs shattered, at the end of a bloody trail. He was beyond speech but out of pain; a glance showed a hopeless case and death was busy with him. A gifted man, Mullen should have landed later with the reserves, but he would not hear of it. No volunteer in the whole brigade was prouder of his beret.'

Piper Millin may have doubled across the canal bridge but at the Orne bridge, which was under equally intense sniper fire, 'I piped over that playing "Blue Bonnets over the Border". The two airborne chaps in the slit trench thought we were crazy because we hadn't taken any notice. But I got over, stopped playing the pipes and I shook hands with the two chaps in their slit trench. Then from across the road

A plaque on the original Pegasus Bridge, now preserved at the Memorial Pegasus Museum, commemorates one of the Commandos killed by sniper fire on the bridge. LCpl Mullen's sketches of the No. 4 Commando action at Dieppe two years earlier remain a superb and evocative record of the attack on the 'Hess' Battery. (WF)

Outside Café Gondrée a plaque to the Special Services Brigade commemorates their critical part in the operation to secure the bridges. The figure of Piper Bill Millin is shown along with the Free French Commando cap badge – Commandos are still in the French order of battle and have retained this distinctive badge. (WF)

appears this tall airborne officer – red beret on. He came marching across, his arms outstretched towards Lovat. "Very pleased to see you, old boy," and Lovat said, "And we are very pleased to see you, old boy. Sorry, we are two and a half minutes late!" We were more than two and a half minutes late but that's the famous words of the link-up of the Airborne and the Commandos.'

In the final hours of 6 June, the men of 2nd Bn The Royal Warwickshire Regiment reached the bridges. Howard briefed their commander and then handed over command of Bénouville Bridge to them, allowing him to lead his *coup de main* party off to Ranville to rejoin the remainder of the 2nd Bn The Oxfordshire and Buckinghamshire Light Infantry. Howard knew he would soon lose 14 and 17 Platoons, who would return to B Company, and so he sent Lt Sweeney forward with a few men to try to find the battalion. Sweeney pushed towards Herouvillette and Escoville for an hour before he met German resistance and fell back to D Company. By 0300hrs the Battalion HQ had been located and, to his great delight, Howard found that Capt Brian Priday, and most of 22 Platoon with Lt Tony Hooper, who had been posted 'missing', were waiting there for him.

ANALYSIS

'Defeat is an orphan,' according to the proverb, 'but victory has many fathers.' In reality, defeat also has numerous parents. The success of Operation *Deadstick* was the result of many factors.

The greatest luxury that Maj John Howard had was time – time to train his men to a very high standard and remove any who were not up to scratch. Time also allowed the force to develop a strong unit cohesion, and for men to learn the strengths and weaknesses of their comrades.

Howard had a simple and flexible plan that every man could understand and know what his role was. Each glider was a self-contained force with its mix of Sappers and soldiers, so that with every glider that landed on its designated landing zone the chances of success increased. However, Howard had also planned for the possibility of the bridges being blown, and assault boats were stowed in the Horsas.

16 JULY 1944

Maj Howard awarded the DSO.

The grave of Lt 'Den' Brotheridge, fatally wounded as he led his platoon across the bridge at Bénouville. The Gondrées added a plaque that explains that Brotheridge was the first Allied soldier to die on D-Day and the distinctive bugle horn is on the right. It is fitting that The Rifles – successors to the Ox and Bucks – have adopted this cap badge. (WF)

LZ-X in 2009. In the foreground is the bust of Maj John Howard with a plinth on the left marking the position where his glider landed. In the background can be seen two plinths where the other Horsas landed. The marshy pond that would claim the life of one of the soldiers is visible in the middle distance. (WF)

The intense and realistic training meant that even though some of the landings – notably that by Chalk 93 – were violent, the men who were uninjured took only a short time before they quickly deployed to their allocated tasks. Men who were less fit and less well-trained would have taken time to recover and orientate themselves; bunched in and around the glider, they would have been an easy target.

The company was sufficiently flexible that when the Ranville Bridge had been secured, 17 Platoon could be redeployed to reinforce the men on the Caen Canal – with the 6th Airborne Division landing, the threat from the east would be greatly reduced.

Howard's choice of a whistle to blow the Victory V signal might have irritated some of the men, who thought it drew attention to the CO and the men around him, making them a target, but it was simple and proved very effective as a rallying signal for the paratroops.

Even when the platoon commanders and in some cases the sergeants became casualties, the close-knit and well-trained platoons continued to function – a product of good training.

Deadstick was not a typically British airborne operation; in many ways it was in the tradition of the German airborne, in which a direct assault is made on a high-value objective. This may run the risk of higher casualties but ensures that the objective is seized. At Arnhem in September 1944 the indirect approach, with men landing on a safe drop zone away from the objective, would lead to failure. If a *coup de main* force had seized the Arnhem bridges and held them until the main force arrived, the outcome of Operation *Market Garden* might have been different.

CONCLUSIONS

On 16 July 1944, FM Montgomery decorated Maj Howard with the Distinguished Service Order (DSO) in recognition of his efforts on the *coup de main* raid. The citation reads:

> Major Howard was in command of the airborne force which landed by glider and secured the bridges over the R. Orne and Caen Canal near Bénouville by *coup de main* on 6 June 1944. Throughout the planning and execution of the operation Major Howard displayed the greatest leadership, judgement, courage and coolness. His personal example and the enthusiasm which he put behind his task carried all his subordinates with him, and the operation proved a complete success.

After D-Day, Howard commanded his company until September 1944, when they were withdrawn from the line. Owing to the injuries he sustained in a car accident in November 1944, he took no further part in the war and was eventually invalided out of the army in 1946. After this he became a public servant until he retired in 1974.

His role in the assault on the bridges was detailed in a number of books and films and after he retired he lectured in Europe and the United States on tactics and on the assault itself. On the 54th anniversary of D-Day, Howard was awarded the Croix de Guerre by the French Government. He died in 1999, at the age of 86.

Years later, Raymond 'Tich' Raynor of 22 Platoon summed up the operation and the reasons for its success. Luck and surprise had been on the side of the *coup de main* force. 'The Germans were not alert. As they had regular bombing raids in that area, they didn't take any notice of the gliders being towed behind the bombers, so when the gliders crash-landed they thought they were bombers crashing. The glider

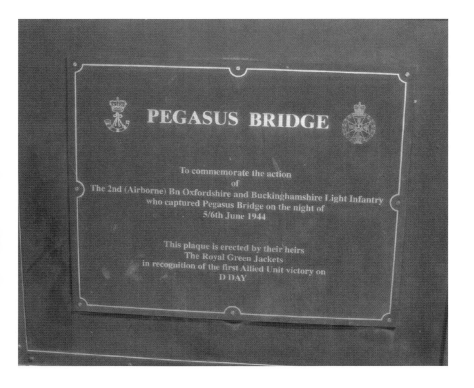

Pegasus Bridge was originally a battle honour for the Oxfordshire and Buckinghamshire Light Infantry. However, in November 1958 the regiment was transferred from the Light Infantry Brigade to the Green Jackets Brigade and became the 1st Bn The Royal Green Jackets. The Royal Green Jackets were in turn absorbed into The Rifles in 2007. Despite these changes, pride in the action at Pegasus Bridge lives on in the new regiment, which has the bugle horn as its cap badge. (WF)

pilots also helped by landing us so near our target. They had been practising for a year on Operation *Deadstick* and the information from the French Resistance and aerial photographs all helped. Sgt 'Wagger' Thornton, without whose PIAT gun all would have been in vain; also Jack Bailey, who knocked out the bunker which John Howard took for his command post; Maj Nigel Taylor of the 7th Parachute Battalion getting his company into Bénouville, and Captain Priday for getting my platoon back to the bridges.'

The *coup de main* operation at Pegasus Bridge continues to be studied by soldiers and military historians. For soldiers the lessons are still relevant – realistic and thorough training, high morale, aggressive leadership and a knowledge that the cause was just and the action critical to the success of D-Day. For many years John Howard was the guest of the Swedish Army Staff College, which during the Cold War studied the operation since they saw key locations in their country as possible targets for a Soviet or Warsaw Pact *coup de main* attack. The author was privileged to hear Maj Howard speak on the exact spot where his glider made its dramatic landing in the early hours of D-Day. As he spoke, the pride he felt for the men of his company and what they achieved was still strong, as was the deep sense of loss for the men who died on D-Day and in the days that followed.

Georges Gondrée died in 1969, the 25th anniversary year of D-Day. Thérèse, his wife, continued to run the café until 1984, dying a few

This superb bronze bust of John Howard by the sculptress Vivien Mallock was presented to the mayor and people of Bénouville by the Airborne Assault Normandy Trust and the Oxfordshire and Buckinghamshire Light Infantry Association in 1994. It illustrates clearly the airborne helmet that on landing was slammed forward over Howard's eyes. (WF)

days after 6 June. The café and surrounding area are now a French national monument, and Mme Arlette Gondrée continues the tradition of hospitality to British soldiers that began in the small hours of 6 June 1944. Hearing Arlette describe the night of 6 June, and perhaps more tellingly, what life under the German Occupation was like for the family, still has the power to captivate the young soldiers who are learning about the 'Realities of War'.

Forty-seven years after the landing, 'Todd' Sweeney returned to Normandy and, escaping from the official ceremonies, visited the Commonwealth War Graves cemetery at nearby Ranville. It contains 2,562 graves, of which just over 2,000 are British and 322 German. Many of these men died in the fighting around the bridges and the drop zones. As the British brought in their dead in 1944 they also collected the bodies of their adversaries and now the Germans rest in their own part of the cemetery. In 1991, accompanied by his former foe, Oberst Hans von Luck, Sweeney returned to honour fallen comrades. 'He went to one corner of the cemetery to mourn his dead, and I went to the other to mourn my dead,' Colonel Sweeney recalled. 'It made me think what war is all about. At the time it was the only way out. But is it necessary? Isn't it a futile way of settling business?'

BIBLIOGRAPHY

Ambrose, Stephen E., *Pegasus Bridge 6 June 1944*, George Allen & Unwin (1984)

Carell, Paul, *Invasion – They're Coming!*, George G. Harrap (1962)

Clark, Lloyd, *Orne Bridgehead, Battle Zone Normandy*, Sutton Publishing (2004)

Daily Mail, *D-Day: The Human Stories* (1994)

Edwards, Dennis, *The Devil's Own Luck*, Pen & Sword (2007)

Ford, Ken, *Campaign: D-Day 1944* (3), Osprey Publishing (2002)

The Godfrey Edition, *Old D-Day Maps: Ouistreham, Pegasus Bridge 1944*, Alan Godfrey Maps (2004)

Howard, John, and Bates, Penny, *The Pegasus Diaries: The Private Papers of Major John Howard DSO*, Pen & Sword (2006)

Howarth, David, *Dawn of D-Day*, Collins (1959)

Lovat, Lord, *March Past: A Memoir by Lord Lovat*, Weidenfeld & Nicolson (1977)

Ramsey, Winston C., *D-Day Then and Now*, Battle of Britain Prints International Ltd (1995)

Saunders, Hilary St George, *By Air to Battle*, HMSO (1945)

5th Bn The Royal Green Jackets, '*Ham and Jam*', Battlefield Study (1 June 1996)

INDEX

Numbers in **bold** refer to illustrations